Praise for

WHAT I DON'T KNOW ABOUT DEATH

"Written in the last months of life, *What I Don't Know about Death* is a deeply nostalgic, insight-filled work of a truly American Buddhism, a heartfelt reflection on one person's journey from an all-American childhood in 1950s Michigan, to India of the 1970s, and on through a life of teaching and contemplation to its heartbreaking end. Sandy Huntington passes effortlessly through the imagined walls between the personal and the academic, weaving a tale from strands of memory, Buddhist thought, literature, and modern life. Just as his in-person teachings and profound conversations did so often, this beautifully written book leaves one floating through a space of emptiness, awareness, and the gentle magic of existence."

—JACOB P. DALTON, University of California, Berkeley, author of *Taming of the Demons*

"*What I Don't Know about Death* is a brilliant synthesis of Huntington's lifelong spiritual and scholarly quest to uncover the truth of what it means to be human. It is one of the finest books on contemporary Buddhism to have emerged from the generation of those who lived and studied in India in the 1970s, then returned home to digest and share what they learned. Completed as the author was dying of cancer, this beautifully crafted and profound work will serve as a lasting tribute to the author's integrity, intelligence, and humanity."

—STEPHEN BATCHELOR, author of *The Art of Solitude*

"Sandy Huntington's *Emptiness of Emptiness* made a seminal contribution to the study of Madhyamaka philosophy in the West. Yet for Huntington, the study of Madhyamaka was not simply an intellectual pursuit. As this book shows, the Middle Way was at the center of his reflections on birth, death, suffering, and liberation, providing a key to his understanding of a life well lived. Following this moving autobiographical sketch, the reader will come to understand why Huntington considered the study of Nagarjuna as 'among the most profound and satisfying experiences of my life.'"

—JAN WESTERHOFF, University of Oxford

"This deeply affecting book represents a poetic distillation of Buddhist insights expressed with a moral clarity and existential vulnerability born from Huntington's own unflinching encounter with dying. That Huntington's last days were focused by the work of thus transmuting that experience, creating from it an essay at once philosophically profound and deeply personal, is a priceless gift—an expression, indeed, of loving compassion."

—Dan Arnold, University of Chicago Divinity School

"This wonderful book is like an easy conversation about the most important matters with a lifelong student of life and death, suffering and joy, and Buddhadharma. Sandy's natural curiosity, which he so generously shares with us, the reader, is perhaps at heart his quiet invitation that we reflect on such things and live in that wonder."

—Geoffrey Shugen Arnold, abbot of Zen Mountain Monastery

"Huntington has given us a parting gift: a profound and deeply personal meditation on the core doctrines of Buddhism; a Dharma teaching on awakening to life in all its pain and exquisite beauty; a poetic and honest text on mortality, spiritual longing, and awakening as love. I will turn to this text in my own teaching, for it overflows with insights and shows us the liberating possibilities of this wisdom of love in our living and our dying."

—William Edelglass, Barre Center for Buddhist Studies and Emerson College

"This book is Sandy Huntington's meditation on his own death, as he was in the process of dying. Its words are pure, to the same degree that the whole exercise is disciplined."

—Francisca Cho, Georgetown University

"What Huntington does not know about death is what we all do not know about death. We do not know what it is like to die. Despite years of avidly consuming books on death and dying, regularly guiding college students as hospice volunteers, serving compassionately as a hospice worker himself, and assiduously researching and writing scholarly works about Buddhist philosophy, Huntington still does not know what it is like to die. Now, though, as he grapples with an unexpected diagnosis of terminal pancreatic cancer, he begins tentatively to touch what he still does not know. Now he begins to see and understand the ferocity of the letting go that is required in order to give rise to the unconditional love that will allow him to die at peace. Through poetry, stories from his own life, his voracious reading of literature and philosophy, and meditations on suffering, desire, impermanence, and grief, Huntington lays out a rich offering to the wrathful deity of death with so much tenderness and humility that all may feel invited to accompany him, as far as we are able, on this most profound journey of life."

—Sara McClintock, Emory University

What I Don't Know about Death

Reflections on Buddhism and Mortality

C. W. Huntington Jr.

Wisdom Publications
199 Elm Street
Somerville, MA 02144 USA
wisdomexperience.org

Library of Congress Cataloging-in-Publication Data
Names: Huntington, C. W., author.
Title: What I don't know about death: reflections on Buddhism and mortality / C. W. Huntington, Jr.
Description: First. | Somerville: Wisdom Publications, 2021. | Includes bibliographical references and index.
Identifiers: LCCN 2021003532 (print) | LCCN 2021003533 (ebook) | ISBN 9781614297505 (paperback) | ISBN 9781614297659 (ebook)
Subjects: LCSH: Death—Religious aspects—Buddhism. | Buddhism—Customs and practices. | Huntington, C. W.
Classification: LCC BQ4487 .H86 2021 (print) | LCC BQ4487 (ebook) | DDC 294.3/423—dc23
LC record available at https://lccn.loc.gov/2021003532
LC ebook record available at https://lccn.loc.gov/2021003533

ISBN 978-1-61429-750-5 ebook ISBN 978-1-61429-765-9

25 24 23 22 21
5 4 3 2 1

Cover design by Jim Zaccaria. Interior design by Tony Lulek.

Printed on acid-free paper that meets the guidelines for permanence and durability of the Production Guidelines for Book Longevity of the Council on Library Resources.

Printed in the United States of America.

To Andy Rotman and David Kittelstrom,
for shepherding this book to publication

Drive

My grandfather used to take
us on summer drives
down Pennsylvania back roads
through bright hot mornings
green with corn that danced along
both sides of our passing
and the sky wide open
as the window I hung out of,
testing the air.

We looked for farms
that nobody lived in anymore.
Not to buy them, just to look.
Not to look, but to see
and remember, I think,
how time passes.
Just to wonder,
how long can you let a thing go on
before there is no going back?

We sat in the car
as the motor ticked and cooled
and we looked at these lost places.

Someone talked, probably—
someone exclaimed about a window
or a weathercock
or pointed out the rusted
tractor by the fallen outhouse
or a tricycle sunken into the yard—
I remember only silence
and the crows calling into it.

Some houses seemed like they
could still be home to someone.
And I imagined it: nails, paint,
soap and water; and a spade
to make the black earth
give something back.
Sheets flapping in the yard;
a child somewhere, crying.

Others were broken open,
their backs hanging
on nothing but memory.
They buckled and sagged into their attics.
They let the clouds slide through.
One leaned and found the limbs of an elm
and then it was a treehouse
for a while.
One was just a cellar hole
with steps leading up into air
and white beeches growing tall inside it
instead of children.

My grandmother got out once
~or did I dream it?~
the car door swinging open
to another life,

my grandfather calling her,
"Edie! Come back!"
as she crossed a lawn,
meadow-high with milkweed,
and found a trellis
half-hidden against the house.
She wrested it from the lilac's green skirts
and brought it back to us,
twisted, rusted,
beautiful with climbing metal roses.
My grandfather helped her
fit it into the trunk.

Now I drive to the summer farm
my grandparents left behind,
pull into what used to be the drive,
now soft with grass,
and cut the motor.

The porches sag.
The barn is gone to sky.
The tangled apple trees
still hold their new, hard fruit:
promises, promises.
The bees hum.
The yellow, summer light falls
on all that brokenness,
those sweet lost dreams.
And no one, ever, coming home
again.

I don't know why I come here
to this empty yard and
these shredded curtains and
the black, watching eyes

of this deserted life
except to maybe hear it
calling back to me,
Hurry,
Hurry,
there is so little time.

Elizabeth Huntington
June 7, 2020

True education consists in this: learning to wish that everything should come to pass exactly as it does.

—Epictetus, *Discourses* 1.12.15

Contents

Prologue

THIS BOOK HAS GROWN out of a lifelong immersion in an ancient vision of the world and of what it means to be human. It is a record of my efforts to learn about and understand my relationship to the doctrines and practices that go under the general rubric of Buddhism. In my professional life I'm a scholar, trained to read and interpret Sanskrit and Tibetan texts from a philological or historical point of view, but in this book I approach Buddhism at an intimate, personal level, attempting as best I can to incorporate Buddhist ideas into my own thinking in a way that pays respect both to my academic training and to indigenous Asian traditions, by taking what they have to say as worthy of sustained, critical attention.

When I began studying Buddhism I was a young American possessed by a need to go in search of a wisdom I was convinced I could not find at home. This search eventually led me to graduate school and then to India, where I lived and studied for years, interweaving what I learned there with what I had brought with me and with events in my personal life as they unfolded. This created from the beginning an unavoidable tension.

As a matter of principle, the classical philosophical and religious traditions of India consider it bad form to lay claim to originality. Nevertheless, in my efforts to incorporate these ideas and practices into my own life I have doubtless interpreted them in ways that would appear foreign to orthodox Buddhist teachers. It was never my intention, however, to simply adopt Asian Buddhist ideas and practices wholesale;

rather my project has always been to understand, as best I could, the ancient teachings, and to bring them into my life as a modern Westerner committed to living within the forms of my own culture, shaped as it is by the intellectual, artistic, and religious traditions of Europe and North America.

I am accustomed to writing for an academic audience; in that kind of writing the aim is to meticulously analyze distinctions unearthed by historical and philological investigation of classical Buddhist texts in the original languages and make arguments about them. This is not my aim here. In this book I'm interested in forging a synthetic understanding based on my own interpretations—interpretations informed both by my intellectual training and my lived experience—of the core doctrines of Mahayana Buddhism as they are found in the Indian tradition and, to a lesser extent, as those same doctrines were adopted and modified in Tibet, China, and Japan. I'm fully aware that in writing from this perspective, without including all the supporting critical apparatus common in academic books and journals, I leave myself vulnerable to the accusation that I may have blurred some important distinctions among various Buddhist schools, texts, and traditions. When taken on its own methodological terms, this accusation merits response. Be that as it may, in these essays I am operating on other terms, with other goals in mind. I have no proposition to defend, and therefore no need to worry about whether what I say here is right or wrong. I am not presenting an argument; I am painting a picture. What may look at times like an argument is better understood as a series of brush strokes on a canvas, for my intention is not to convince but to inspire. I want to inspire my readers to look deeply into themselves and into the world where they live and dream. I want them to look beyond thought, beyond belief, beyond hope and expectation, desire and fear, beyond even imagination. I see this book not as a rational analysis or explanation of Buddhist philosophical doctrine, much less as a reasoned argument in support of my approach to reading Buddhist literature. Rather, this book is best viewed as an exhibition or showing of that approach—an attempt, that is, to put this particular way of reading on display along with the peculiarly intimate form of truth it makes available. In this respect this book is a continuation of work I began with the writing of my novel, *Maya*.[1]

I am a voracious reader of contemporary philosophy and literature, both of which have profoundly shaped the writing of this book. In my view, poetry and fiction offer a wonderfully nuanced hermeneutical lens through which to appreciate the psychological sophistication of Buddhist ideas and practices. Critical reflection, logic, and rational argumentation play an essential role in generating intellectual conviction or belief, and they have factored heavily in the development of Indian Buddhist thought; but intellectual conviction and belief are not in themselves sufficient catalyst for the type of radically transformative "unknowing" that characterizes Buddhist awakening.[2] What is ultimately required, in my view, is a sensitivity for the metaphorical underpinnings of all language—including the language of reasoned argument with its implied search for objective, literal truth—a point I will return to at intervals throughout these essays.[3]

In addition to fiction and poetry, the Hebrew Bible and the writings of certain Christian authors have also been useful to me, despite the fact that my own relationship with Christianity has been spotty. I was raised Methodist, but after my parents left the church when I was around twelve, I never looked back. Then, somewhere along the line after graduate school, I experienced a growing interest in theistic religion. It may have been the influence of living in India for all those years: exposure to the "philosophical God" of Vedanta, to the aesthetic radiance of Kabir's devotional poetry, or perhaps to the sheer exuberance of the Hindu pantheon. My interest in theism may also have grown organically out of the necessity, at the small liberal arts college where I teach religious studies, to place myself in meaningful conversation with my students, most of whom identify as Christian. Whatever the case, over the years this interest in Christianity has blossomed, fed primarily by my discovery of a whole new world of enchanting literature. I'm not only referring here to modern classics like the fiction of Leo Tolstoy and Fyodor Dostoevsky, or to the mystic eloquence of the medieval apophatic tradition that led from Dionysius the Areopagite through St. Augustine, St. Bonaventure, and Meister Eckhart to *The Cloud of*

Unknowing. I also have in mind contemporary authors like Denys Turner, David Bentley Hart, and the Pulitzer Prize–winning novelist and essayist Marilynne Robinson—all of whose work is a palliative for anyone who finds the New Atheists and their scientism intellectually superficial and grindingly tedious.[4]

My students frequently ask if I am Buddhist. I usually respond by explaining that, through some obscure karmic dispensation, I've spent my adult life studying and practicing Buddhism, but I do not call myself Buddhist. This hesitation implies no judgment whatsoever about Westerners who identify as Buddhist. Here, as in other ways, my outlook has no doubt been deeply—and perhaps (I'll freely acknowledge) perversely—influenced by the writings of the Buddhist philosopher Nagarjuna. Nagarjuna is a connoisseur's skeptic; his work articulates the apex of skeptical thought in a tradition noted for its commitment to skepticism, to letting go of all dogmatic formulas and labels and of every definition of the self. To read Nagarjuna in the original Sanskrit has been among the most profound and satisfying experiences of my life.

Finally, I should say something about the title of this book, and about the book's recurrent evocation of death. For me—and, as I believe, for Buddhist traditions in general and perhaps for all religions—death casts a long, dark shadow over human affairs, raising questions that defy any simple, formulaic response. And yet, all the while, the existential reality of our predicament as self-conscious, mortal creatures continues to press in from all sides in a way that makes it impossible to ignore. Contemplation of death—*memento mori*—is central to any spiritual path.

As I write these words, we are, all of us, struggling to come to terms with a worldwide pandemic. Death has unexpectedly gripped our communal imagination. Apart from the pandemic, and speaking in the most personal of terms, a great deal has changed since I began work on this book. Not long ago I was diagnosed with terminal cancer. I have, most likely, less time than I would prefer to set my affairs in order. And so, with due respect to the British philosopher Christopher Hamilton, I do not, in this moment, feel wholly or even sufficiently insulated from the tragedy of life.[5] When it comes to death, I no longer have the luxury of writing at a distance. Or not much of a distance, at any rate. Nevertheless, as Martha Nussbaum has suggested, "writing about the beauty of human vulnerability is, paradoxically, a way of rendering oneself less vulnerable, and more in control of the uncontrolled elements of life."[6] I will have a bit more to say about this later, but I feel my present circumstances ought to be acknowledged up front, given the subject of this undertaking.

In the final analysis, one might say that this book explores a particular kind of truth at once religious, philosophical, and literary, a way—one way—of seeking to live authentically in the face of our limited time on earth. Insofar as this seeking entails an ethic of self-surrender at the very deepest levels of human experience, it offers, I believe, a welcome counterbalance to the unapologetic individualism and greed that infects so much of contemporary society.

What I Don't Know about Death

I KNOW NEXT TO nothing about death.

It's not as if I never had any opportunity to learn. In Michigan, where I grew up, the first thaw of early spring regularly draws back the curtain on a gallery of small, frozen bodies, the partially decomposed remains of mice and squirrels and sparrows scattered in a tangle of twigs and leaves and cigarette butts and crushed soda cans and the sodden pages of last year's magazines. Detritus from another journey around the sun. There would as well have been a parade of weightless corpses dangling under sinks or in the shadowed corners of our attic and basement. All of this would have been on show, plainly visible to any child with eyes to see. Enough, certainly, to provoke what Nietzsche once called "the great suspicion." But my first memory of death is not of these countless, simple markers found everywhere in nature; rather, it is of a stunningly cruel act of genocide, the ruthless execution of an entire population of innocent lives.

I can track this event back to the first half of the 1950s, which makes it one of a handful of my earliest memories. I would have been around five or six years old. At that age, the sense of myself as a conscious agent was only just beginning to take hold. Possessed of a great curiosity about the world and a burgeoning interest in science, I was anxious to wield what little authority I had in order to pry my way into nature's secrets. It was one of those stifling hot, late July afternoons in the Mid-west, when the cicadas buzzed in the trees like miniature chainsaws and mothers hydrated their children with grape Kool-Aid, refilling their plastic mugs from a pitcher stored in the Frigidaire. I had spent most of the afternoon in our backyard, on my hands and knees, catching grasshoppers. It's not difficult. You simply cup your hands around their stiff green exoskeletons and scoop them up. You can feel their angular legs pumping frantically there in the darkness, tickling your palms as they struggle to get free. I found plenty of them—enough to fill one of the mason jars my mother used for making jelly from the cherries my sister and I pulled from the branches of the tree behind our house. When the jar couldn't hold any more grasshoppers, I tightened the lid and brought it to the back stoop, setting it down on the cool, shaded concrete, where I could closely inspect my captives. My hands were stained with their saliva, brown smears of "tobacco juice."

I don't recall whether what I did next had been part of the original plan. The idea may have come to me as I watched the grasshoppers impotently kicking against the shiny glass walls of their prison. I do have a clear memory, though, of standing beside the stove, waiting for the water to boil. And I remember carrying the hot kettle outside, the smooth Bakelite handle nestled against my palm, the wooden screen door slamming behind me. I remember carefully unscrewing the lid, steam burning my knuckles as I filled the jar with scalding water. I remember being fascinated by the grasshoppers wriggling and squirming, how they flexed their powerful legs, how it took several minutes before they quit fighting and finally grew still.

This was the beginning of my early career as an assassin. I soon discovered that there were as many ways to kill as there were moths and spiders and other small creatures to be killed. Which is to say, the possibilities were endless. For the adults—whom I closely observed—it was enough to thoughtlessly crush the little bodies under the heel of a shoe, or attack them with the fly swatter we kept hanging on a hook in the kitchen closet, next to the broom and dustpan. But for a small child overflowing with curiosity, there were other, more creative and engaging ways to take these seemingly insignificant lives. One could easily pass an hour, for instance, hovering over an anthill with a magnifying glass, carefully bringing the intensely focused point of light to bear on one insect after another, watching each one sizzle and curl, their legs folding in on themselves. If I listened very closely I could hear a faint crackle, like the sound made when my mother stripped the cellophane wrapper from a package of Lucky Strikes and crumpled it between her fingers.

In those days all the boys I knew had BB guns. I had a Daisy pump-action one that I carried with me in the autumn when my father and my uncles went pheasant hunting, all of us tramping together among rows of dried cornstalks, their parched yellow leaves rustling against our arms and legs, the mist of our breath taking shape in the crisp autumn air. My uncle Keith's two spaniels ranged ahead, close to the earth, moving in a broad arc. While the men patiently waited for a bird to panic and hurl itself up into the sky, my cousins and I worked the edge of the meadow near the woods, shooting indiscriminately at anything we saw. Songbirds, mostly—sparrows and goldfinches and red-winged blackbirds perching in the bare branches of the trees. When the BB struck, they would flutter for just a moment, then drop like ripe fruit. Often they would still be alive when they hit the ground, beating their wings uselessly against the leaves while we finished them off with a few more shots fired at close range.

Every summer during my elementary school years I stayed for a few weeks with my grandparents in the small Michigan town of Eaton Rapids. They lived just blocks away from Horner Woolen Mills, an abandoned factory on a bank of the Grand River. A three-story complex of crumbling red brick, broken timbers, and vacant, shattered windows. My cousin Greg and I passed whole afternoons roaming the hallways that opened on either side into cavernous rooms lined with long metal tables and gigantic industrial machines bristling with corroded gears and pulleys. By that time we had graduated to CO^2 powered pellet guns and found there was an endless supply of rats scurrying provocatively in and out of sight.

During the days leading up to the Fourth of July, fireworks began to appear. Teenagers with cars would drive down to Ohio, where such things were legal, returning with a trunk load of contraband explosives. The slim cylinders of Black Cats could be shoved down the throats of snakes and turtles who were then turned loose, fuses hissing between their thin lips as they fled for safety. You could drop waterproof Cherry

Bombs and Silver Salutes off the bridge, down into shallows near the bank of the river, where they erupted in a furious geyser of brown water, flinging the mangled bodies of carp and smallmouth bass several feet into the air. The boys who did these things were the same boys who delighted in hunting frogs with darts. I was present for all of this. I watched but was repelled by what I saw. Shooting at a moving target was one thing; this, evidently, was another. What most bothered me was their laughter. These boys did not seem to understand that death was a serious business.

The period of my innocence—if such it had been—ended abruptly one summer afternoon between sixth and seventh grade. I was roaming the woods near my home, my weapon slung over one shoulder, when I spotted a squirrel climbing up the side of a broad oak tree. I raised the rifle and shot. A pellet gun can't easily kill an animal that size, but the shot nevertheless penetrated the squirrel's flesh. It lost its grip and skidded down several feet, then managed to sink its nails into the bark and frantically pull itself upward. I fired again, and once more the squirrel faltered, slipped down a foot or so and dug in, climbing strenuously upward, slower now but still determined to escape. I took several more shots before it finally let loose, dropped to the ground and lay there twisting and raking at the earth. Where the pellets had entered, the fur was torn and matted with blood. I stood and watched life ebb away. The little jaws opened and closed, releasing a trickle of red saliva that formed a small pool at my feet. At last the squirrel's head jerked back in one final violent exertion, and it lay still.

This was certainly nothing new. By then I had witnessed the death of dozens of small creatures. But for some reason, this time, I did something I had never done before: I went home and told my mother. I found her sitting at the kitchen table, drinking a cup of tea, a basket of laundry at her feet. She listened quietly as I described what had transpired. When I finished she did not immediately respond. But when, after what felt like an immense silence, she at last spoke, I was shaken by the anger and disappointment in her voice. *You should be ashamed. I'd like to go down to the woods and find that poor squirrel and bring it back and put it right in the middle of your bed.*

Is it possible she hadn't realized, until that afternoon, what I was doing all those years with the guns? Did she imagine this was the first time I'd murdered a small animal for no other reason than to watch it die? And why, on this particular occasion, did I suddenly feel it necessary to confess? I must have known how she would respond. Maybe I needed to hear her angry words in order to confirm what I had myself been suspecting. Whatever my motive, by the time my mother finished speaking, I knew the killing was over. I stashed the guns in a back corner of my closet, out of sight, and never touched them again.

Until then death had been an object of fascination, an intricately cut jewel that I held carefully between two fingers, turning it this way and that as the light skimmed across its surface. Taking these small lives was a way of engaging with death while still keeping it at a safe distance, a declaration of my own strength. But now, on the brink of adolescence, I had for the first time caught a faint glimpse of my image staring back at me. There was something wrong here, something far beyond the scope of my influence. Something I could neither understand nor evade.

During these same childhood years, I witnessed a string of naturally occurring deaths. First the loss of several hamsters, all of them named Hammy. Hammy 1 and Hammy 2 died at night, burrowed down in the cedar shavings. We found Hammy 3 stiff and cold, huddled in one corner of the cardboard box where he had been sleeping. Each of these small bodies was wrapped in a swath of cotton from my mother's ragbag and dutifully buried under the hedge in our backyard. There was a chameleon I purchased from a man at the Barnum and Bailey circus; it had barely stirred at the end of its fine silver chain before I noticed, the day after I brought the poor creature home, that the slender, scaled body gripping my shoulder was lifeless and rigid.

And there was Stanley, an Easter chick from the Kresge discount store. Every spring several dozen such chicks would appear, weightless balls of fluff dyed various shades of pastel pink and green and blue, crowded together in a glass aquarium lit from above by a single bare incandescent bulb. Remarkably, Stanley survived and grew into a fat white rooster that perched on his cage in our heated garage next to my father's magnificent, gleaming Buick Electra 225. For quite a while a few pink feathers peeked out here and there from under his adult plumage. Much to my delight, Stanley crowed every morning at sunrise. Later in the day he busied himself around the yard surrounding my parents' suburban home, strutting up and down the drive under the basketball hoop or pecking and digging for bugs in the manicured grass. He developed a close relationship with Schnitzel, our miniature Schnauzer; the two of them liked to nap together in the afternoon sun. As it happened, Stanley's trust in this alien species—his natural predator—turned out to be ill advised. One afternoon I returned from high school to find him prostrate in the ditch near the mailbox, eviscerated by a neighbor's dog.

But the death I remember most vividly from my late childhood was the passing of our dog, a boxer named Toby. Toby was mine long before Schnitzel arrived on the scene. He was there waiting when my parents brought my infant self home from the hospital. For all I knew Toby had been living with my mother and father since the beginning of time. I grew up in his company; he was my ever-present companion, my confidant, and my solace. Together we explored the woods that bordered our neighborhood, with its mysterious, beguiling creek. On hot summer afternoons we dozed in the shade of the lilac bushes that grew in the backyard near an old apple tree.

A black and white Kodak snapshot survives from this period. My mother must have taken it, probably in 1955 or '56, just in front of my father's treasured rose bushes. He is there in the picture with Toby and me, dressed in loose-fitting, pleated slacks and a tight white t-shirt, his dark hair combed back in a glistening pompadour. He was in his mid-thirties. Young and untroubled by time, he grips the wooden handles of a wheelbarrow in which Toby is sitting hunched precariously forward on his front paws, his jowls drooping, his sad eyes patient and trusting amid the folds of skin. I'm standing next to them, a barefooted boy in khaki shorts and a plaid cotton shirt neatly tucked in at the waist, looking out at the camera with a quizzical smile. One hand rests lazily on Toby's back, just behind his shoulders.

In the summer of 1959 my family moved to an affluent neighborhood on the west side of town, and everything in my life was suddenly different. I had to adapt to a new school, find new friends. Within a month of the move, Toby was dead. One hot afternoon in early September, his ailing heart seized, and he collapsed, panting, in the living room of our fancy new home. He died there, sprawled on the deep-pile powder-blue wall-to-wall carpeting, and my childhood died with him.

What I encountered with Toby's death was something new. No longer a mere physical event, or an object of contemplation held at bay, here was something dark and obscure and frightfully real. The presence of an absence. A bleak, meaningless, empty silence; a stark token of our unceasing defeat at the hands of time.

My earliest conscious encounter with human mortality came in elementary school. At the time my family still lived in East Lansing, within walking distance of Michigan State University. We hadn't yet moved across town. In those days I often rode my bicycle on the university campus, and one of my favorite places to visit was the museum of natural history. As I left behind the bright sunlight and passed through the stone arch at the museum's entrance, I was engulfed by a sudden stillness, by the odor of forgotten things and lost lives preserved. Most days I headed immediately to the lower level, descending a polished marble staircase that spilled into an eerie subterranean realm of dimly lit hallways, each one lined with meticulously constructed dioramas that depicted the lives of North American Indians and other indigenous peoples. A series of cabinets displayed prehistoric human encampments, whole worlds hermetically sealed behind plate glass and mysteriously illuminated from within. I don't remember ever seeing another living person in those halls. I was alone, moving from one glowing showcase to the next, captivated by the miniature figures of men hunting, women cooking over tiny fires, gangs of children engaged in undecipherable games—all of them motionless and mute, eternally fixed in what would otherwise have been just another moment on a day like any other.

But the real treasure in this museum—my ultimate destination—was situated at the juncture of three hallways that converged around a single glass case. Inside this case was the mummified body of a young girl wrapped in the tattered folds of a funeral shroud. Judging from her size, she had been perhaps six or seven years old at the time of her death. If she were alive, the two of us might easily have been friends; in a sense, we were. I found her mesmerizing. Her feet, two shriveled stumps of leathery flesh, protruded from one end of the blanket. Her arms were drawn up and folded across her chest, the tendons in her wrists and the backs of her hands stretched tight under dull yellow skin. Nails sprouted obscenely from the tips of her fingers and toes like long, curling claws. Her eyes were closed, as if she were lost in some ancient reverie, her thin lips pulled back in a feral grin.

It was around this time, when I was in fifth grade, that I first experienced the death of someone close to me. My mother's father collapsed in the basement of his home in Asheville, North Carolina, while shoveling coal into the furnace. Madison Stuart Hodges was an honorable, aristocratic gentleman, someone who displayed the kind of manners often associated with the South. Everyone in the family, including his grandchildren, called him "M.S." My grandmother found him down there in his vest and bow tie, sprawled on the floor next to a broken-down wheelbarrow, his fingers still gripping the shovel. His coat had been carefully folded and hung over a banister. The iron door of the coal burner was open, and light from the flames must have flickered across his face.

I have a vague memory of my mother speaking into the receiver of our heavy black phone, talking with Mama—that's what we all called her mother—in urgent, hushed tones. I knew something terrible had happened, though I could not grasp precisely where the terror lay. Within hours we had packed our suitcases and loaded them into the trunk of the car. There were no interstate expressways then, and the drive from Michigan to North Carolina was a series of two-lane highways meandering through the dark Midwestern countryside, through the villages and towns of Ohio and into the hills of Kentucky and Tennessee. We drove all night in my father's big Buick sedan; my sister slept stretched out on the back seat under a blanket while I curled up on the floor, my legs arched over the hump in the carpet where the driveshaft passed through. I remember the steady hum of tires against the pavement, the warm air from the heaters under the seat. And I recall something of my grandparents' house, the formal portraits on the wall, my parents dressing for the funeral, my grandmother in a black pillbox hat and veil. At the funeral home my mother led me to the enormous metal casket. The upper half of the lid was open, tilted back so I could see the quilted satin lining. Standing there holding her hand, I was just tall enough to peer over the edge to where my grandfather lay so alarmingly still, wearing his old-fashioned suit and delicate, rimless glasses, his hands folded neatly across his chest in a way the made me think of the mummy girl.

My mother's mother went next. Ollie Irene Barrough Hodges. Mama. She had been visiting us in Michigan when she slipped on the icy stairs in front of our home, fell, and broke her hip. After that she continued to decline both physically and psychologically. The last years of her life were spent in a convalescent home—that's what they were called in those days, when such places were relatively rare. The place where my grandmother convalesced was a stately Victorian mansion with carefully tended gardens, its long, sloped lawn stretching to the banks of the Grand River. There, among the ornate polished furniture and the regular chiming of a grandfather clock, she slipped through a hidden doorway into a world of her own, a place inaccessible to the rest of us. She recognized no one, nor did she speak. Still my mother visited her several days a week, sat by her side for many long years, and stroked the thin strands of her silver hair until death finally took what little remained.

After that it was Laverne Huntington, my father's father. I must have been around sixteen when he died. In my memory, he is a slight, taciturn man in rumpled gray workpants and a flannel shirt, sleeves rolled up to his elbows. Except on Sundays, when he went to church with my grandma. Then he wore a dark brown suit and fedora. Not one of those raffish little things that Frank Sinatra was famous for, tilted back high over his forehead; my grandfather's hat had gravitas. It was a 1940s model made of wool felt that had grown soft after a decade of use in sun and rain and snow. The brim was substantial, the front dipped slightly downward, and the back edge had a gentle upward curve.

In the years immediately following their marriage, he and my grandmother owned a small farm, but the land was repossessed by the bank during the early years of the Depression. The horse, a few cows, and most of the tools were sold at auction. They took what remained, along with their four young children, and moved into town, where the family did whatever they could to make money. My grandfather worked as a day laborer and, later, as the local distributer for the Detroit Free Press. Eventually they saved enough money to purchase a dump truck, and he contracted with a nearby gravel pit to make deliveries. As children, my cousins and I loved to ride in the back of that truck, perched atop a load of sand as we sped along Michigan's back roads. Grandpa slipped imperceptibly out of my life while I was busy with school and friends, with meeting girls, with my rock band and motorcycle. I looked up briefly and found that he was gone.

All the years I was growing up, my father's mother—Gladys—was either weeding the garden out behind their house or in the kitchen cooking. I seldom saw her without an apron. Dinners were pot roast or honey-glazed ham with mashed potatoes and vegetables from the garden. She would get the water boiling and send me out with a bucket to fetch corn. I remember snapping the ears off the tall stalks, pulling back the translucent green husks, the even rows of yellow kernels cool and smooth and damp against my fingers. There was always a pie on the kitchen counter—cherry or apple—and a crockery jar filled with chocolate chip cookies. In the mornings of my summer visits, she served up an endless succession of blueberry pancakes. Grandma lived long enough to see me through college and into a first, brief marriage and a series of adventures in Europe. I worked on a farm in Norway, taught English in Greece, got divorced, began graduate school, and at twenty-five went off to India for four years to study Sanskrit. I returned to Michigan just in time to see her through her dying. The scene played out in the emergency room of a small rural hospital, where she lay attached to a ventilator on a gurney under a bank of bright, antiseptic lights. She would never again breathe on her own. In the adjoining room, my father and his siblings sat around a table trying to decide what to do. When my father suggested that the tube be removed from her throat, his younger brother accused him of wanting to murder their mother. All of this took place in the late 1970s, when the medical technologies that prolong our dying were only beginning to emerge and conversations like this were something new.

As it happened, my father would be the next one to die, only five years later. By that time I was in the final stage of graduate school. I had a Smithsonian grant that allowed me to return to India for research on my dissertation, and I was scheduled to leave just after Christmas. For some months he had been experiencing increasing difficulty just getting around. He was in constant discomfort and now walked only with the help of a cane. Through it all, the doctors had insisted he was suffering from arthritis. Then, in late November—only a month before I was scheduled to fly to New Delhi—the results of a biopsy showed that he had multiple myeloma, a form of cancer that begins in the marrow of the bones and metastasizes from there to the blood and kidneys and lungs. At the time of the diagnosis, my parents were preparing to leave for a tour of art historical sites in China, but they were forced to cancel their plans so my father could begin treatment. Neither my mother nor my father was prepared to accept the reality of the situation. In fact, no one in my family was able to fully comprehend the seriousness of his condition. To return the grant and curtail my research plans was clearly not on the table; doing so would have been to admit the gravity of my father's illness, and that was precisely what none of us were willing to do.

And so, early on a cold, snowy morning in the first week of 1984, I found myself standing in my parents' kitchen with my bags packed, ready to leave for Detroit Metro airport. My father was wearing his flannel pajamas, a dark blue rayon bathrobe, and slippers. He walked slowly across the room, leaning on his cane, gripped my hand in his, and held it. Our eyes met. He was sixty-seven years old, already stiff and frail from the effects of the disease, but his graying hair was, as I recall, still combed in place. He spoke some words of encouragement, wished me success in my research. Such was the nature of our charade that I did not allow myself to think: *I'll never see you again, Dad. I'll never again hear your voice. I'm leaving you here to die.* Nevertheless, over the course of the next year, cancer would turn him inside out with pain before finally bringing him to ruin. By the time my family contacted me and

I returned from South Asia, the funeral was over, his ashes relegated to an urn. Dust to dust.

My mother was devastated, enraged at the cruelty and injustice of the world, that a good man who had never done anyone any harm should suffer as he had suffered. She descended into a vortex of loneliness and misery from which she never emerged. Like her own mother had done almost thirty years before, she left us behind and took up residence in a place beyond the reach of our feeble sympathy. A year passed in this way, and then one night while visiting my younger brother in Baltimore, she went to sleep and never woke up. She too was cremated. I never saw her corpse, and I have no memory of the last time we were together. She simply vanished from my life without notice. I and my siblings buried her ashes along with my father's at the foot of a red maple on the campus of Michigan State University, where my father had spent most of his working life. The tree had been paid for and planted at our request, as a memorial, but owing to some local ordinance, we were forbidden to inter the ashes on public land. We performed this last rite surreptitiously, in the early evening on a weekend when no one was around to wonder what these four people were doing out behind the administration building, crawling around on their hands and knees with a shovel and two small urns. A year later the tree contracted a fungus, and the grounds crew dug it up with a backhoe, roots and all. They carted everything to the dump and planted another maple in its place. We might as well have scattered our parents' remains over the Baltic sea.

Since that time the losses have steadily mounted. All my aunts and uncles are now gone. Both sides of the family—an entire generation—erased. A few years ago my dear friend Karl died, seven months after being diagnosed with an aggressive thyroid cancer. More recently my father-in-law succumbed to congestive heart failure. Before they entered my life, these men were already husbands and fathers, someone's son and someone's brother. They had friends and colleagues, active lives in the community. They went out to dinner and to the theater, read books, argued, and laughed. And now the curtain has fallen on all of that, the sorrow and the joy are finished, and what remains is only so much as pliant memory permits.

These days my life feels more than ever like a dream, fleeting and ungraspable. What time remains to be lived is nothing compared to what has gone before, and what has gone before is now a raft of fading recollections, unmoored and drifting in the luminous void of the mind.

Madison Stuart Hodge's Seth Thomas clock sits ticking on the mantle, marking off the minutes and hours and days, as it has been doing for over a century. The pendulum swings in its predictable arc, ratchets catch and release, a maze of delicate cogs turn and mesh. Once a week I rest my left palm on the curve of the oiled mahogany cabinet, loosen the brass latch, and swing back the convex glass that shields the dial. I do what my father did, what my mother's father did before him, place my hand where they placed theirs, feel the same worn brass key between my fingers. All over again, I tighten the coiled steel that will drive this fragile mechanism another few days.

> The thing that hath been, it is that which shall be;
> and that which is done is that which shall be done:
> and there is no new thing under the sun.[7]

What shall be is the people close to us shall die; and what shall be done is death shall take them from us at any moment on a day like any other. This much I know, but it is a knowledge that has entirely to do with the death of others and so is next to nothing compared to what I do not know. What I do not know about death has to do with myself.

And that, now, is what I must learn.

It's evening, late in what has been yet another long day of living with my illness. I lay my hand on the banister and tentatively climb the stairs. The hinges of my knees complain but nevertheless do their job, flexing and bending, lifting this freighted soul upward one step at a time. In the bathroom the bemused face of an old man looks back at me from the mirror. The line of his jaw has grown slack, his skin is flushed, coarse, and weathered. A delicate net of purple veins ornaments one nostril. His forehead and neck are marred by repeated applications of the dermatologist's scalpel—moles, skin tags, lesions, cancers. Layers of the self peeled away, fathomless depths of pretense exposed to the light.

The relentless accumulation of experience no longer holds the charm it once so carelessly offered. And still, like those grasshoppers kicking vainly against an invisible barrier, I instinctively resist death's call, this ineluctable giving over of the self to a greater truth, consummated in the flames of love and grief.

The Life and Death of the Buddha

For although you may not believe it will happen,
you too will one day be gone.

GAUTAMA, PRINCE OF THE SHAKYAS, was destined from birth to become the Buddha. His mother, Queen Maya, dreamed that a tiny, vaporous white elephant descended effortlessly into her womb. Some months later the infant emerged, luminous and immaculate. Seven days after that, we are told, the queen died in the throes of an unbearable joy.

Thus begins the ancient story, as recounted in the second-century poet Ashvaghosha's epic Sanskrit poem *Life of the Buddha*.[8] And yet, apart from the extraordinary circumstances of his birth and, later on, a few cameo appearances by lesser deities, most versions of the biography agree that Prince Gautama's life was largely devoid of miracles or the kind of visionary experiences often taken as the defining trait of mysticism. As presented by Ashvaghosha and the Pali-language *suttas*, or discourses, the Buddha never denies the possibility of supernatural events or powers, or exotic visionary experiences, but he consistently maintains that they have little to do with his teachings and that concern with such things can become a diversion from the difficult work of spiritual practice.

Notwithstanding the wonders that attended his birth, the prince who became the Buddha was entirely human and vulnerable to a panoply of human afflictions. He is important for us not because he transcended his humanity but because he burrowed so deeply into our common plight. In doing so he learned more about the pain of being human than most of us would care to imagine. Perhaps more than we could bear.

According to legend, shortly after the Buddha was born, an astrologer told the prince's father that the boy could grow up to be a powerful monarch—the mightiest ruler ever known—or he would renounce the world in order to pursue the life of a spiritual pilgrim. Were the latter to happen, the king's son would achieve universal renown as a wise man, a teacher and guide for others. Based on the astrological circumstances of his birth, it was impossible to know for certain which path his life would take.

Anxious to ensure that his boy would grow up to inherit the throne, the king devised a plan. First, he provided the prince every possible luxury. As a small child he was entertained and indulged; as he grew older, he was kept busy. His attention was constantly directed toward mastering the skills necessary for success in the world or toward gratifying his senses. If the young prince could not be kept entirely happy and preoccupied, he was at least taught to assume without question that life's purpose and happiness lies in doing and having, achieving and owning.

Here is our first important clue about the nature of the spiritual life as presented in this story: it is rooted in discontent and requires the kind of leisure that affords space for reflection on questions of meaning and value. The king obviously understood this, which accounts for his strategy: keep the prince occupied with practical affairs, and if at all possible, keep him happy. This way it will never occur to him to seriously question anything about the circumstances of his life.

Most of us begin life wrapped in a cocoon of innocence, even if we don't remain in it for very long. Unless born into a world of proximate violence or harsh poverty, a young child is to some extent unmindful of what might be called the disagreeable truths of life—its existential terrors and uncertainties, all those elements of existence that flourish outside the parameters of our will, embodied above all in the ever-present specter of death. This is not to deny the dark sides of a child's psyche, with its own inherent fears and anxieties, only to suggest that for many of us there was a time in life when the greater understanding of our predicament as mortal creatures was relegated to the wings, when center stage was occupied with the delights and discoveries of a new world and its extravagant and seemingly endless wonders. Many parents want to keep it this way, at least for a while. We delight in our children's innocence, in the vision of life that it embodies, and we mourn its inevitable loss.

I was born in 1949 and grew up with all the optimism and comfort of a white, middle-class American life, surrounded by men who had fought in Europe or somewhere in the Pacific and were anxious to put that experience behind them. When they weren't working hard at making a living, the adults seemed to move from one party to the next. Nobody talked about the war. My father's army uniforms and medals were packed in a trunk stored up in the attic, out of sight. But in one corner of our living room, on a small shelf of books, someone had left a hardcover copy of the *Life's Picture History of World War II*. I passed many hours as an elementary school child sitting alone, transfixed by the glossy black-and-white photographs of human bodies tortured and maimed, corpses sprawled on the earth, hanging on barbed wire or stacked by the hundreds in trenches alongside the road. The pictures were graphic, but they were still only pictures. And then, without warning, death suddenly moved closer.

There was my grandfather's body at his funeral, lying in the open casket, meticulously groomed and consumed by a strange, unearthly stillness. He had become one of *them*. One of those people in the pictures.

How fragile is our happiness. How ultimately futile our struggle for control.

Prince Gautama is in his mid-twenties, married and with an infant son of his own, when he asks his father for permission to leave the palace grounds. Why should this man-child want to escape the idyllic life of the palace? Why do children yearn to grow up? For many the desire may be rooted in a fantasy of omnipotence that adults appear to embody. To be an adult suggests, from the child's perspective, the possibility of total, uncompromising power along with the freedom to indulge one's every whim. For the prince it may be mere boredom or curiosity, a simple, unfocused thirst for something new. To be trapped on the palace grounds—no matter how extensive and luxurious—is nevertheless to be trapped. This suggests a subtle, discomfiting fact about pleasure, how the persistent gratification of desire brings in its wake an inevitable ennui.

The poet tells us that Prince Gautama has heard rumors of the enchanting qualities of the city's parks and groves and desires to see them for himself. The king reluctantly agrees to his son's request, and before long the day of his first outing arrives. The road leading to the municipal gardens has been cleared of anything that might upset the delicate sensibilities of this young man who, until this moment, has been kept ignorant of the suffering of the world. When his chariot passes through the palace gates, people are crowded along the way, eager to see their future king. As fate would have it, however—or, in Ashvaghosha's telling, as the gods arrange—a decrepit old man emerges from the crowd and stands in plain view, shrunken and feeble, hunched over his walking stick. One can imagine the encounter:

"Who is that person?" the prince asks his charioteer. "Why does he appear this way, so very distressed?"

"My Lord, he is broken by old age. He was once an infant, then a small child. But time has stolen his strength and beauty, withered his senses, and addled his mind."

"Is this condition peculiar to this man?"

"No indeed, my Lord. It is not."

"Will old age befall my wife?"

"Yes, my Lord."

"And my infant son? What of him?"

"He too, my Lord, will become like this in the course of time."

"And I as well? Is this my destiny?"

The charioteer nods.

"Take me back to the palace. I've seen enough for today."

Three more outings follow, each one bringing with it another revelation. We know the story, and even if we didn't, we could guess. The second time out Gautama sees a sick man, the third time, a corpse. And on each occasion he asks the same questions, receives the same answers.

On his fourth and final trip outside the palace, the prince rides unannounced to a remote spot in the country, waves away his guard, and sits alone in the shade of a rose apple tree, watching an impoverished farmer till his field under the hot sun. The man is caked with grime and sweat. He goads his ox with a stick, striking the beast's ribs to urge him along. The plow leaves behind a trail of mutilated insects and worms. How, Prince Gautama wonders, can people find any real pleasure in life when old age, sickness, and death are our common fate? The months and years pass so quickly, and everything ends in loss.

As he sits quietly reflecting in this way, he is approached by a wandering ascetic. He looks up to find the man standing only a few feet away.

"Who are you?" the prince inquires. "What do you want?"

"I am a man, like you," the ascetic responds, "a man who once lived among family and friends. But all that is finished. Fearful of birth and death, I left that life behind in search of release from this perishable world. I no longer want the things other men want. I sleep where I can, in a deserted temple, under a tree in the forest, surviving on alms I receive from others."

Prince Gautama resolves, in this moment, to leave the palace for good.

The world outside the palace is the adult world. Our world. A world at once intimately familiar, captivating in its endless complexity, and appallingly burdened with sorrow. It is a world where a woman in her mid-sixties loses her husband—the love of her life—to bone cancer. She watches him struggle with unrelenting pain that eventually collapses into death. Left alone, her heart broken, she is so overcome with anxiety and depression that she dies in her sleep within a year. It is a world where a boy with cerebral palsy is bound in a wheelchair, slumped forward, the weight of his chest pulling against the straps that hold him upright. He registers no clear sign of thought or emotion and cannot speak to his mother and father, who must see to his care every moment of the day and night. It is a world where a blood vessel is about to burst in a man's brain. A forty-year-old father of two small children, exercising in a local gym, will lose his grip and tumble sideways off the treadmill. He will be dead before he hits the floor.

> Man that is born of a woman hath but a short time to live, and is full of misery. He cometh up, and is cut down, like a flower; he fleeth as it were a shadow, and never continueth in one stay.
>
> In the midst of life we are in death.[9]

To speak of such things is depressing. Our modern sensibilities rebel. After all, why dwell on the negative? The world includes both pleasure and pain, ugliness and beauty, so why not focus on what pleasure and beauty there is and, as much as possible, ignore the rest until we're forced to deal with it? This is perhaps how the most fortunate among us live—or try to live. *Carpe diem!* This is the way the king of the Shakyas wanted his son to live. At this point in our story, however, such a life is no longer possible for Prince Gautama, who has become a desperate man. Desperately vulnerable, we might say, and completely incapable of returning to his old life in the palace. To do so now—after what he has seen—would be to live a lie. The lie is that there could be, in such a life, for such a person as the prince, any happiness at all. "Hard indeed," he exclaims, "must the hearts of men be, that they can perceive such truths and yet find pleasure in this world."

Each of the first three times Prince Gautama left the palace, his initial concern was with the suffering of a stranger, then, on reflection, with the suffering of those close to him, and finally with himself. On his fourth trip out, he was overwhelmed with compassion not only for the farmer but also for his ox, and for the insects and worms crushed by the plow. The unease that drove him to leave the palace was not simply distress in the face of his own inevitable aging, sickness, and death; it began and ended with an anxiety about the suffering of others. A "hard heart" is a heart that has closed itself off from the world in order to pursue a life of pleasure that is fundamentally selfish and thus permeated with self-centered fear.

Here we begin to sense the deeper meaning of the story of the Buddha's life as an allegory for the spiritual path. For the prince, who has now, in his desperation and despair, abandoned his wife and child to the care of his father and left the palace, sorrow does not simply alternate with or overshadow life's joy; for him what is typically experienced as joy, or pleasure, is at this juncture no longer even possible. His own family has become for him a source of pain, and in his anguish, he will become a source of pain for them. Here we begin to see that the work of spiritual practice is a messy, agonizing business. The problem Prince Gautama is wrestling with is not merely a form of existential angst—anxiety, that is, about the difficulty of finding happiness in one's life when happiness is seen to be so very tenuous and fragile, when it could be stolen at any moment by accident or disease. When it *will* be stolen, inevitably, by old age and death. The problem the prince faces is as well a moral problem, exemplified in this question: How can I find happiness for myself when the happiness of others—those people I care about—is every bit as tenuous and fragile as my own? Even if the circle of my care extends no further than my family and friends, my vulnerability in this regard is nevertheless inescapable. And if, like the prince, I were to find myself in sympathy with the plight not only of my family and friends but of all human beings—or all sentient creatures—what then? So the real question he faces is not about happiness at all. The real question is, can a life lost to suffering—one's own suffering and the suffering of others, which have become indistinguishable—be somehow redeemed? The prince's crippling malaise lies at the heart of the spiritual path.

No one is entirely immune to this malaise. Though we may succeed, most of the time, in pushing it aside by staying busy with the day-to-day concerns of work and family and social life, a residual anxiety always threatens to force its way through the façade of happiness. And so we search for ways to manage that anxiety. Psychotherapy or psychiatry, with its access to ever more powerful mood-altering pharmaceuticals, is an increasingly common path. Many people find solace in the religious tradition of their parents, in going to church or synagogue or mosque. For others, the chronic dis-ease of life propels them to search beyond their inherited religion to classical philosophers and contemporary gurus, to the study of theology or to exotic contemplative practices. This was the path taken by Prince Gautama after he abandoned the palace. For the next six years he traveled from one teacher to the next exploring India's ancient wisdom, the philosophy of Sankhya and the teachings of the Upanishads, and received instruction in meditation.

There is a particularly stark image of the prince at this stage in his journey, a statue dating from the second century CE now housed in a museum in Lahore, Pakistan. Gautama is shown seated in the classic lotus posture, his body emaciated from months of starving himself. His face is skeletal, his eyes set deep in their sockets, his lips compressed in a grimace, the veins in his forehead are distended. It is difficult to imagine a more powerful depiction of a self fiercely struggling to live with the burden of an immense and undeniable anxiety. A self that wants nothing more than to be rid of itself.

After six years of searching, of listening and learning from others, the prince left his teachers. There was no more to learn, no one, at this point, who could help him. He had reached a dead end, unable to live with the truth he had seen, and unable to put it out of his sight. In the writing of St. John of the Cross, this stage in the spiritual life is characterized as "the dark night of the soul." He walked aimlessly for several days, wandering through the countryside near the old city of Gaya, and finally sat down to meditate at the root of a pipal tree. What happened late that night is a great mystery—the central mystery of Buddhism. But the message conveyed by the story of Prince Gautama's life is clear enough.

The attempt to find happiness by ignoring or minimizing the truth of aging, sickness, and death ends by stunting our humanity, rendering us unable to live with authenticity and grace. In our fear of loss, we fear the grief that accompanies love, and so we fear love itself. If, however, we can find the strength to open our hearts both to the complexities of our own suffering and to the unbearable sorrow of the world—which are not truly different—then life becomes increasingly susceptible to the wonder of a renewed innocence. As David Bentley Hart has it,

> Wisdom is the recovery of innocence at the far end of experience; it is the ability to see again what most of us have forgotten how to see, but now fortified by the ability to translate some of that vision into words, however inadequate.[10]

In a life so redeemed nothing is wasted. Even the most trivial details take on unexpected significance.

Is such an all-embracing acceptance of life and death possible? The British philosopher Christopher Hamilton believes that it is human nature to wish to transcend the conditions of our mortal existence, which would mean that we are trapped in a fundamental contradiction. As Hamilton puts it: "If you accept yourself, you will accept your longing to escape your condition, and therefore seek to do so; if you do not accept your condition as a human being then, similarly, you will seek to escape your condition. Either way you're caught."[11] Perhaps we can learn to accept precisely this: *we are caught*. Perhaps in accepting this much—really accepting it, with no escape into rationalization or dogma—we may glimpse a kind of rare, precious freedom, the freedom to live with what we are given, without reservation.

This, at any rate, is where the story ends. The prince, now eighty years old and widely recognized as a great spiritual teacher, was sickened by a scrap of bad pork given to him as alms by some pious citizen. He had no strength left to fight the illness, which quickly took its course. In the final moments he lay on his side, closed his eyes, and slipped away. We are told that he died at peace, reconciled to a seemingly obvious truth he had spent the last forty-five years of his life repeating endlessly to anyone willing to listen, as if there were something in these words—some urgent message—that in our busy lives we fail to assimilate no matter how many times we are told: *change is the only constant; what is born must die*.

The story is so very old, but the Buddha's final teaching is everywhere echoed in the writings of saints and novelists and poets; contemplation of our fleeting existence is the gateway to all deeper spiritual truths. In our own time, with his poem "Notice," Steve Kowit has passed the ancient message on to us in language that is both thoroughly contemporary and timeless:

> This evening, the sturdy Levis
> I wore every day for over a year
> & which seemed to the end
> in perfect condition,
> suddenly tore.
> How or why I don't know,
> but there it was: a big rip at the crotch.
> A month ago my friend Nick
> walked off a racquetball court,
> showered,
> got into his street clothes,
> & halfway home collapsed & died.
> Take heed you who read this,
> & drop to your knees now & again
> like the poet Christopher Smart,
> & kiss the earth & be joyful,
> & make much of your time,
> & be kind to everyone,
> even to those who do not deserve it.
> For although you may not believe
> it will happen,
> you too will one day be gone.
> I, whose Levis ripped at the crotch
> for no reason,
> assure you that such is the case.
> Pass it on.[12]

Dis-ease

Those who will not slip beneath
    the still surface on the well of grief,

turning downward through its black water
    to the place we cannot breathe,

will never know the source from which we drink,
    the secret water, cold and clear,

nor find in the darkness glimmering,

  the small round coins,
      thrown by those who wished for something else.[13]

ACCORDING TO THE BOOK of Genesis in the Hebrew Bible, after laboring for six days to create the world, God looked out over everything he had made and saw that it was very good. I believe this is what most of us want. We want to feel that this world is very good—or at least basically good. But our desire runs up against a grim and complex reality, aptly characterized by Ernest Becker in this passage from his book *The Denial of Death*:

> What are we to make of a creation in which the routine activity is for organisms to be tearing others apart with teeth of all types—biting, grinding flesh, plant stalks, bones between molars, pushing the pulp greedily down the gullet with delight, incorporating its essence into one's own organization, and then excreting with foul stench and gasses the residue. Everyone reaching out to incorporate others who are edible to him. The mosquitoes bloating themselves on blood, the maggots, the killer-bees attacking with a fury and a demonism, sharks continuing to tear and swallow while their own innards are being torn out—not to mention the daily dismemberment and slaughter in "natural" accidents of all types: an earthquake buries alive 70 thousand bodies in Peru . . . a tidal wave washes over a quarter of a million in the Indian Ocean. Creation is a nightmare spectacular taking place on a planet that has been soaked for hundreds of millions of years in the blood of all its creatures. The soberest conclusion that we could make about what has actually been taking place on the planet for about three billion years is that it is being turned into a vast pit of fertilizer.[14]

Becker's question resonates: In this world, where life feeds on life, an individual sentient being in itself seems to be of no ultimate worth. It has been said that nature values the *idea* of the individual but not any *actual* individual. How are we ever to find rest in such a world?

The truth is our experience is anything but restful. This is not to deny life's pleasures, those fleeting moments of satisfaction when circumstances temporarily cater to our desires. But we spend our days, for the most part, drawing lines between the acceptable and the unacceptable, embracing what we will and rejecting the rest. We judge and choose, fret and worry. And with good reason. As individuals, and as a society, we recognize real problems that need to be addressed, things that need to be fixed—though the solutions may be far from obvious. Creation may not be a "nightmare spectacular"—though it undeniably is for many—but even the more fortunate would agree that there is plenty of room for improvement. Despite centuries of human labor to remedy the psychological, sociological, and biological ills that make our existence here a continuing struggle, the suffering mutates and persists, much of it the direct result of our own shortsighted political or technological machinations—to say nothing of the human capacity for brazen cruelty, often enough justified as a means toward some common good.

A suspicion arises that there may be, after all, some structural flaw at the center of things, some ugly defect that can never be erased, nor repaired, nor explained away. To make matters worse, a big part of the problem is, of course, not "out there" but rather "in here"—inside our own minds and hearts, which conceal an astonishing number of disturbing fantasies and desires. It can feel, in our less guarded moments, very much as if something were fundamentally wrong not only with the world but with us, something that we cannot and should not accept, much less love. This suspicion, however, is too much to bear, for it threatens to plunge us into a bottomless well of grief "turning downward through its black water / to the place we cannot breathe." So we avert our gaze and get on with our day-to-day lives, making—in the words of T. S. Eliot—the best of a bad job.[15]

Prince Gautama, on his way to becoming the Buddha, could not avert his gaze. His encounter as a young man with aging, sickness, and death triggered a spiritual crisis that propelled him to abandon the pleasures of palace life. His six years of study and contemplative practice culminated under the Bodhi tree in an insight that he later conveyed in the form of a medical diagnosis. Human beings, he declared, are ill, and the symptom of our illness is our inability to find a home for ourselves here in this world as it is. We are subject to a chronic malaise that infects everything we experience—even what we most desire, what passes for happiness. This is the first noble truth, the bedrock of Buddhist doctrine and practice. *Dis-ease* (*duhkha*) is our disease. Seeing this truth for ourselves, in our own experience, is where the Buddhist path begins.

To appreciate what is involved here, one must see how it's possible to be ill without realizing it. The early signs of cancer can easily be written off as incidental aches and pains. Recognizing and acknowledging the symptoms of my illness for what they are is the initial, indispensable step toward a commensurate cure.

The distinction between dis-ease—a spiritual affliction—and mundane, unavoidable pain is easiest to discern in our experience of physical discomfort. Years ago, as a college student, I waited tables at a restaurant where the head chef was a big man who routinely bullied us all with the force of his physical presence. One day while chopping shallots he nicked a finger. I happened to be picking up an order when the accident happened, and I saw him lift his hand and hold it there, staring with obvious distress at the cut. A tiny drop of blood beaded where the tip of the razor-sharp blade had grazed his finger. He examined it for a moment, his face paled, and he dropped to the floor, unconscious.

There is the physical sensation of pain, and there is our dis-ease *about* the pain—an existential distress that accompanies and can actually dwarf the physical sensation. Buddhist teachings suggest that this holds true for psychological as well as physical pain: a similar agitation is present whenever our experience runs counter to our desires. When I don't get what I want, or when I get what I don't want, I become restless, worried, fearful. That is to say, I want to be happy, so when I'm unhappy, I'm not only unhappy, I am also anxious *about* my unhappiness.

Less obvious, but equally pervasive, is the dis-ease that emerges when what begins as pleasure merges imperceptibly into pain. In my sophomore year of college I bought a sports car—a Triumph GT6. A dark blue fastback with wire-spoke wheels and a dashboard made of real, polished wood. The car rode so low to the ground that at a stoplight I could hang my arm over the open window and stub out a cigarette on the pavement. I had to work hard to make the monthly payments, but the pleasure I got out of driving this racy British machine made it worth the effort. Or so it seemed, for a while. This was the late 1960s. American cars were enormous. My little British roadster was hard to spot from the cockpit of a GTO or a Camaro—much less from the driver's seat of a Buick Electra 225 like the one my father drove. Parking lots were particularly dangerous places. Several times I returned to my car to find a gash in the fender where someone had backed into it. Whenever this happened I would take it to the body shop for repairs. One time when the car was parked, a passing stranger wantonly snapped off the antenna, which I replaced—what's the point of having the perfect car when its perfection is marred? All of this was of course expensive. I was working at a restaurant where the boss was a jerk and the schedule so tight I didn't really have enough time to study for my classes. The pressure of keeping up with school and job was intense, but for months I stuck with it. Until one day I had an epiphany.

I was out for a drive, alone, listening to Simon & Garfunkel on the eight-track tape player. I had stopped at an intersection, and just a few feet in front of where I sat with the engine idling, two undergraduate girls were crossing the street. One of them tossed her hair back carelessly, blond curls flashing in the sunlight. She was laughing and preoccupied with their discussion and clearly took no notice of me. But I noticed her. And I noticed that neither of them noticed me. And what's more, I noticed that I cared. But why, I reflected, should they look at me? And why should I be upset if they don't? And yet I *was* distressed. I wanted very much for those two girls to acknowledge me sitting there in my shiny British sports car. In fact, I *needed* them to look. When I realized all this, a curtain was momentarily drawn back, permitting me an insight into the role the car played in my life. It was supposed to be making me happy by enhancing a particular image of myself that I desperately wanted to project, but it had in fact become the source of a great deal of anxiety. The cost of maintaining this self-image was suddenly crystal clear. I felt very lonely and, in my loneliness, both sad and absurd.

When the traffic light changed, I drove directly to the bank and asked what I owed them, went from there to a used car lot and sold the Triumph for exactly that amount, then hitchhiked back to the bank and paid off the loan. I went from there to the insurance company and canceled my policy. All of this was accomplished within the space of a few hours, and the sense of relief was extraordinary. It was as if I'd been set free from prison. I'd been stressed out for months but hadn't been willing to admit it to myself—or even to *see* it. That night I had my shifts at work reduced by half.

A trivial example, but it's an experience I've never forgotten. This was a few years before I encountered Buddhism, but in that moment at the stoplight, I glimpsed the lineaments of a principle with much broader application.

We can become so focused on the *idea* of pleasure that it takes a while to realize that whatever pleasure might originally have been there has long since morphed into pain, and we may not be able to pinpoint when the transformation occurred. Moreover, by the time we acknowledge the truth, chances are we have already turned our attention to some new fantasy of happiness. So the cycle continues, flourishing as it does on our near boundless capacity for denial.

Sigmund Freud saw denial as a basic coping mechanism, a strategy of the ego to protect itself from any perceived threat to its integrity. Sustained marital conflict, drug or alcohol addiction, compulsive behaviors surrounding money or food or professional status, the exercise of unearned social or economic privilege—anything that might make us feel vulnerable or guilty can in principle be denied. When confronted with a situation too uncomfortable or threatening to accept, the ego rejects the empirical facts, insisting that whatever it is could not be a problem despite the presence of prodigious evidence to the contrary. Denial differs from a straightforward refusal to accept what is seen to be true; for to be in denial means that I simply do not see the truth. It is to Freud's credit that he illuminated the unconscious mechanism of denial and showed how it operates below the radar, allowing us to live with what would otherwise be unbearable.

But how deep does our denial reach? How much of life is unbearable?

"The closer you look, the more clearly you see that denial is part of the uneasy bargain we strike to be social creatures." So says Michael McCullough, a psychologist at the University of Miami.[16] Becker goes even further. He views the whole of American society as engaged in a silent conspiracy to deny the fact that our desperate search for happiness is permeated by an unremitting terror of impermanence and death.

Which brings us to the subtlest level of our dis-ease, referred to in Sanskrit as *samskara-duhkha.*

According to Buddhist teachings, both unhappiness and happiness are infected by our dis-ease. As I discussed above, when we are unhappy, we are not only unhappy, we are also anxious about our unhappiness. A similar principle holds true for happiness: we are anxious because our happiness is never all that we want it to be. At the very least, we are attached to our present happiness and we want it to last, even though we know from experience that it won't. (As Allen Ginsberg once observed, every marriage harbors an implicit question: *Who will die first?*) But we are seldom conscious of the residual anxiety caused by our attachment to present happiness. In fact, what we take for happiness is so tenuous and fragile that it can only exist in a state of denial, an implicit commitment to not consciously acknowledge anything that might destroy the illusion and reveal the depth of anxiety just below the surface.

If you doubt what I'm saying, let me suggest a modest exercise. Next time you're feeling happy—let's say at a social gathering, enjoying good food and conversation with friends—take a moment to think about something that makes you sad or stressed. Something significant. You can think of your ailing mother, lying alone in a nursing home, or of the millions of people around the world who are at this moment innocent victims of misogyny, racism, or political violence. Think about global warming, or about that dark, irregular mole on your thigh that seems to have appeared out of nowhere. It doesn't take much reflection to come up with something disturbing. There's never any shortage of things out there capable of upsetting our happiness. Once you have found your unhappy thought, dwell on it.

This can be an edifying experiment in two ways. First, if you're able to follow through with it, then you'll see just how easy it is to spoil your good mood, which shows you how superficial it was to begin with. Being happy is like walking on a thin layer of ice stretched over an abyss of frigid darkness. One needs to tread carefully, barely lifting the feet, in order to avoid falling through. And that's precisely what we do. If we're fortunate enough to be happy for a while, we tread very cautiously. Which means, above all, that we don't *think* about how carefully we're treading and how much anxiety that constant vigilance generates. Which is why it is doubtful anyone would actually perform the exercise I've recommended, even if they chanced to remember it.

No matter. Even if you don't do the experiment, you can still see how easy it would be to make yourself unhappy, and how the refusal to challenge your happiness in this way is itself evidence of denial. Simply contemplating the experiment one learns something important about the nature of pleasure.

Samskara-duhkha is a form of anxiety etched indelibly into the structure of the personality. It is an existential or, perhaps better, a spiritual disorder, a dis-ease that permeates my identity as an individual person—which is to say, my entire psychological life. Merely to exist as an individual, to identify with a particular set of memories and traits, hopes and dreams—to think *this is me, here I am doing such and such, exercising my preferences, pursuing my goals*—is to be dis-eased. This truth is hidden from view behind a cloud of denial, which periodically allows for the illusion of happiness. Certainly we learn to accept that life is far from perfect and that it brings times of sadness and even despair; but Buddhism's first noble truth goes much deeper. We do not see—nor do we *want* to see—how everything about our experience in this world, including our pleasure, is inherently dis-eased. This is the truth about what it means to be a self-conscious, self-centered individual, and our resistance to seeing and accepting this truth is literally built into our identity. Denial, in this sense, is the groundwork of the personality, the bulwark of my sense of myself as one person set apart from others. We find it virtually impossible to admit—as Prince Gautama did when he left the palace—that our hard-won moments of happiness are a charade. It is simply too much to bear.

Denial always comes at a price, however, and the cost of not facing up to the truth of our dis-ease is high. It requires a formidable reservoir of psychic energy to maintain the pretense of even a periodic, ephemeral happiness. The difficulty of breaking through denial is in direct proportion to the significance of the truth that is buried. To see how the car I wanted so badly had become a source of anxiety took some time, but it was relatively easy. To see that my marriage is hopelessly dysfunctional—or that I'm an alcoholic, or that I hate a job I can't afford to quit—is considerably more difficult, for it may demand that I reappraise my entire life from the ground up. But even that is a relatively simple task compared to what we're dealing with at this third, and most subtle, level of dis-ease. To see how I am by my very constitution as a self-conscious individual condemned to suffer is another thing altogether, for it places an unconscionable burden on the psyche. No wonder Buddhism teaches that this most subtle form of dis-ease is perceived only at a relatively advanced stage of the spiritual path when attachment to the sense of self has already become so attenuated that one no longer resists such an insight.

The characteristic response of denial, when confronted with the truth, is anger. *This can't be what Buddhism teaches. It is simply too bitter a pill to swallow.* In any case, what is called for is not belief. Buddhist literature includes numerous cautionary parables about the dangers of merely believing—as opposed to critically reflecting on—the teachings of the Buddha. Belief alone is not only insufficient in these matters; it can easily itself become a hindrance to going deeper. Ultimately, one must look for oneself and see the workings of *duhkha* in one's own experience. I must see for myself whether dis-ease is the water I swim in, the air I breathe. This is where the spiritual path began for Prince Gautama, which is no doubt why, as the Buddha, he made the pointing out of disease the subject of his first noble truth.

The more I wriggle and squirm, scheme and strategize to get what I want, the more hopelessly dis-eased I become. Thomas Merton has eloquently captured this fundamental principle:

> Indeed, the truth that many people never understand, until it is too late, is that the more you try to avoid suffering, the more you suffer, because smaller and more insignificant things begin to torture you, in proportion to your fear of being hurt. The one who does most to avoid suffering is, in the end, the one who suffers most: and his suffering comes to him from things so little and so trivial that one can say that it is no longer objective at all. It is his own existence, his own being, that is at once the subject and the source of his pain, and his very existence and consciousness is his greatest torture.[17]

But when the nature of my illness—the quiet desperation of the isolated, individual self, striving to be happy—is unearthed, brought into the light of awareness and clearly seen for what it is, then this very seeing lays the foundation for a cure.

Thirst

> Without, the night was cold and wet, but in the small parlour of Laburnam Villa the blinds were drawn and the fire burned brightly. Father and son were at chess, the former, who possessed ideas about the game involving radical changes, putting his king into such sharp and unnecessary perils that it even provoked comment from the white-haired old lady knitting placidly by the fire.

SO BEGINS *The Monkey's Paw*, W. W. Jacobs's orientalist fantasy originally published in England in 1902.[18] Since its appearance over a century ago, his story has cycled through myriad printings and been adapted for stage and film, for opera, comics, and television—including an episode of *The Simpsons*. It continues to capture our interest because this unassuming fable illustrates, in a vivid and compelling way, a deeply troubling dimension of human desire.

The family is expecting a visitor—an old friend, sergeant-major Morris, who has recently returned to England after serving in the British army in India for twenty-one years. When he arrives, the four of them settle in by the fire for whiskey and tea (the tea, presumably, for Mrs. White), while Morris, with some prodding, speaks of his adventures in the exotic East. He is distinctly reserved. From the first, we sense that this "burly, rubicund" man is concealing a mysterious psychic wound.

When his host, Mr. White, expresses a yearning to go to India himself, to see "the old temples and fakirs and jugglers," the sergeant-major responds laconically, "Better where you are." The conversation eventually turns to a discussion the two men had a few days earlier, during which Morris commented in passing on a curiosity he had carried back from India—the mummified paw of a monkey. And now, as they talk, he removes the grotesque object from his pocket and holds it up in the flickering light of an oil lamp.

> "It had a spell put on it by an old fakir," said the sergeant-major, "a very holy man. He wanted to show that fate ruled people's lives, and that those who interfered with it did so to their sorrow. He put a spell on it so that three separate men could each have three wishes from it."

The conviction that there is a mysterious, implacable order underlying our experience here in the world has widespread and ancient roots. Humans from disparate cultures dating back to the dawn of history have believed the circumstances of our life are preordained in some sense we can never quite grasp, so that the only real freedom anyone ever has is the freedom either to affirm what is given or to struggle against it, in vain.

Thy will be done, on earth as it is in heaven.[19]

A striking contemporary illustration of this attitude was provided by the Amish community's reaction to the brutal murder, in 2006, of five Amish girls in a rural Pennsylvania schoolhouse. One of the parents told a syndicated reporter, "We believe it is all part of God's plan. It's up to us to pick up our lives and move on." For a modern secular rationalist, such radical, unquestioning acceptance of a tragedy like this is virtually inconceivable, if not abhorrent in its apparent passivity. What kind of God would endorse the slaughter of five children? And why should I simply *submit* to the will of such a God, without protest? Nevertheless, quiet surrender to "things as they are" remains a common ideal of many religious traditions. The Book of Job in the Hebrew Bible is a classic example, but the same attitude characterizes the spirituality of the

Qur'an and the Bhagavad Gita, as well as the oral traditions of native North American and other indigenous peoples. Our task in life is to accept gratefully—or at least without complaint—what we are given, even when it is far removed from what we might desire.

The immediate reference in Jacobs's story is to the Islamic idea of *kismet*; but the mention of fate in this context suggests a number of associations relevant to our understanding of Buddhism's second noble truth, according to which human suffering stems from our unquenchable thirst for more or for something other than what is given in present experience. According to Buddhist teachings, our fear of aging, sickness, and death is only an inverted, mirror reflection of this incessant craving. For beings like us, even the most pleasant of circumstances can always do with some improvement. Nothing we are given is ever quite good enough, if only because it can and ultimately will be lost.

Any child's first response to hearing about a wish-granting monkey's paw would be to exclaim *Wish for more wishes!* And who wouldn't, if they were clever, and if the paw had not come with its own restrictions. But then, is that really what we want—to keep on wishing, forever? Do our desires really have no limit? The previous owner of the paw, we are told, used his third and final wish as a means to suicide. In response to a question from Mr. White's son Herbert, Morris acknowledges that he used all three of his wishes, but he declines to say what they were. As if, perhaps, his experience with the little severed hand had taught him some important lesson. *Better where you are*. But who is going to listen to such advice? Where I am is never as good as where, in my fondest dreams, I could be.

And then, without a word, Morris pitches the little paw into the fire. Mr. White quickly rakes it out of the flames. He admits to being attracted by the mystery of the thing, though he himself has no idea what to wish for. In response to his son's protest, he mumbles, "It seems to me I've got all I want." Nevertheless, goaded on by Herbert, he wishes for two hundred pounds—enough to pay off the mortgage on their home. As he does so, the paw twists ominously in his hand.

Like Mr. White, even when we are inclined to admit that we have all we really need, we're nonetheless easily tempted to wish for something more. According to Buddhist teachings, this unappeasable thirst is both the cause and the immediate manifestation of the chronic dis-ease that infects everything about our present experience. As Terry Eagleton puts it: "Desire is an anonymous field of force into which we fall as into a sickness, a monstrous fatality or ontological malaise into which we are born and which chooses us far more than we choose it."[20]

At the most obvious level, this "thirst for more" appears as a craving for physical comfort or pleasure, or for material goods that offer the promise of ease and sensual gratification—the sort of things that money can buy. A lucrative industry of advertising, state-sponsored lotteries, and consumer culture is built on the sophisticated manipulation of our yearning for some physical or psychological consolation beyond what we presently enjoy. Mr. White's first wish was an expression of this kind of apparently innocent desire: just enough money to pay off the mortgage. But the seeming innocence of his wish is belied by the macabre reality of the shriveled paw that squirms in his hand like a snake.

The next morning over breakfast, before Herbert goes off to work, there is some good-natured chiding about Mr. White's credulity. And yet, it's clear that neither Mr. White nor his wife can quite dispense with the business of the wish. The couple begins a long day of waiting and watching—against their better judgment—for they know not what.

Late that afternoon a stranger appears outside their door—a messenger, it turns out, from their son's workplace. He tells them that there has been a terrible accident at the factory. Herbert was caught in the machinery and killed. The firm admits no liability, "but in consideration of your son's services they wish to present you with a certain sum as compensation."

Two hundred pounds.

Obviously neither comfort nor pleasure is simply a matter of acquiring more. There is always a desire not only to enhance but to preserve what comforts we already enjoy, or to reclaim those that have been lost. One way or another, we go on wishing. This urge to have and hold can play itself out in countless subtle ways. For example, we are irresistibly attracted to abstractions—ideas and ideals—that embody and reinforce our need for security and stability. Any religious, political, or economic doctrine that caters to recognized cultural norms can become the focus of this thirst for the continued existence of the status quo, this deep resistance to change. Unfortunately, it's all too clear how even the noblest ideals, when enshrined as an end in themselves, have often in the course of history been enlisted as justification for reprehensible violence. In this context one thinks immediately of the crusades or the inquisition, but also of a comment made by Vladimir Putin on the U.S. war in Iraq, which he characterized as "exporting democracy on the tip of a Tomahawk missile." We seize, sometimes to the point of fanaticism, on ideals that hold out the promise of maintaining or reclaiming an altogether imaginary security.

Herbert's mutilated corpse is buried, and the old couple retreat into mourning, shattered by the loss of their son. Ten days pass in this way, and then one night, Mrs. White is roused from sleep by a revelation: *the paw*. She shakes her husband awake. "Go and get it and wish!" Mr. White is horrified. He tries to dissuade her. At the funeral she had refused even to view the mangled body of their son. What if Herbert were to return now in some ghastly, distorted form? *Wish!* she cries again. He capitulates to her demand, retrieves the paw from where they left it downstairs, and makes a second wish. Once again it writhes in his fingers and drops to the bedroom floor.

Faith in the eternal life of an individual soul that survives the death of the body or in an omnipotent creator God who stands outside the flux of time can function as expressions of our resistance to change. We *want* to believe—against all evidence to the contrary—that there is something in our experience that endures, something solid and recognizable that we can rely on for support. Nor are such beliefs the sole property of religion. The altogether secular, quasi-scientific idea of "matter" as the metaphysical ground of reality nowadays functions as an article of unreflective faith for virtually everyone except quantum physicists, who—at least as professionals—know better. Similarly, it would never occur to most of us to seriously question the commonly held belief that a person's name is attached to a real, individual self—the "me" that endures over time, moving through life from birth to death, accruing experiences as it passes unchanged in essence from one birthday to the next. In Jacobs's story this kind of desire characterizes Mr. White's second wish—that his son would be resurrected, that he would continue to live. A desire to reverse or correct what an earlier desire brought to bear. One desire piled on top of another.

They wait, and wait. The hours pass, Mrs. White maintaining a vigil by the window. Long past midnight they go back upstairs and lie in bed, exhausted, awake in the dark house, listening to the ticking of the clock and the scratch of a mouse's tiny feet as it scurries through a wall.

Just before dawn it comes: a faint knock at the door.

> "It's Herbert!" she screamed. "It's Herbert!"
>
> She ran to the door, but her husband was before her, and catching her by the arm, held her tightly . . .
>
> "For God's sake don't let it in," cried the old man trembling.

Whatever is outside is now violently pounding on the door. Mrs. White breaks free of her husband's grip and undoes the lower bolt. Now she is climbing onto a chair, straining to reach the bolt on top. Mr. White, in a panic, clamors back up the stairs to their bedroom, drops to his knees and searches for the monkey's paw. He finds it where it had fallen, snatches it up, and makes his wish.

Mr. White's third and final wish is for his son to die.

The particular thirst associated with this wish is referred to in Buddhist texts as "the thirst for nonexistence." It can manifest as anything from an elaborate, intellectualized defense of nihilism or atheism to a brute, inarticulate impulse to suicide. Whatever its expression, it is the inevitable corollary of our earlier clinging to what we have: "the thirst for nonexistence" is a longing to be rid of what our previous desires have wrought, a hunger for release that emerges when it becomes evident that the very things we most desired were also the source of our deepest grief. In this respect, the thirst for nonexistence carries with it a glimmer of understanding, the suggestion of an insight into the veiled nature of desire in its most subtle and seductive guise.

Thirst is always coupled with ignorance, which in Buddhist terminology refers to our failure to perceive the way in which everything about our present experience is, as a matter of existential fact, fundamentally conditioned or—as I've been saying—given. Christopher Hamilton draws attention to this disconcerting truth:

> You did not choose to be born or where to be born. Nor did you choose your parents or your siblings, if you have any. You did not choose your sex, or your mother tongue or your physical characteristics, and you did not choose the basic features of your character. Nor did you choose the socio-economic class or group into which you were born or the basic opportunities and difficulties that were placed in your way as you grew up. Virtually nothing at the beginning and in the early years of your life was yours to choose. Moreover, throughout life this continues to be so: the people you meet, the interests that you develop, the place you end up living in and much else besides: all of this is largely a matter of luck or chance, good or bad. Further, you have no choice about the fact that the world, your world, is a world which matters to you in various ways, is a world with which, and in which, you are engaged.[21]

Hamilton calls the power that directs our lives "luck" or "chance." Buddhists call it karma. There are obviously important semantic nuances to the words, but the underlying principle is clear: I have no jurisdiction over the essential circumstances of my life and death. Contrary to what Hamilton seems to imply, however, the influence of luck or chance, or karma, or fate—or whatever you want to call the governing principle behind the appearance of self and world—is unrestricted. Even if my present reality is shaped by choices made in a past life—as Buddhism would have it—that reality nevertheless confronts me now as a *fait accompli*, entirely determined by forces beyond my current knowledge or control. And my previous life (if there was one) was identical in this respect. The contours of my experience are invariably and ineluctably *given*. What we call "choice" is a mere epiphenomenon, a play of light across the surface of vast, hidden depths of unknowing.

But (one might object) doesn't this contradict our experience? Hamilton is obviously right that much of life is not in my control, but certainly there are crucial junctures when I actually make choices and decisions. Am I not then exerting my will so as to shape circumstances in conformity with my own desires?

An unquestioned belief that I have the power to make choices is the central conviction—the primary article of faith—on which rests my entire sense of myself as the master of my destiny. Formally articulated in the doctrine of free will, some version of this belief plays a central role in some strains of biblical theology and in a sizeable swath of post-enlightenment Western philosophy. Though it takes many more or less nuanced forms, this belief can be expeditiously reduced to a simple metaphor: There is a tiny homunculus ensconced somewhere in my skull, perhaps in the region of the pineal gland. Call it "the soul," if you like. He or she or it sits there like Captain Picard at the helm of the starship *Enterprise*, looking out through my eyes at the world, issuing commands that result in words and actions that in turn have real consequences for myself and others.

Make it so.

A metaphor of this sort goes hand in hand with the primal thirst to be in control not only of the circumstances of my life but of myself as well. Dogmatic faith or reasoned conviction in one or another version of free will could in this respect be read as an embodiment of Buddhist ignorance, the intellectual counterpart to our unquenchable thirst. It is the primal metaphor that undergirds the story of the monkey's paw and makes it so captivating.

Nevertheless, *wanting* to be in control is not the same as actually being in control. Nor does the mere belief that "I am in control" make it so. From the Buddhist perspective, any given choice or decision is the result of an infinitely complex, interlocking web of antecedent causes and conditions, some of them biological or evolutionary, others social or historical—including, if you will, the influence of countless previous lives. In any case, no choice or decision is entirely unconditioned, the free and arbitrary act of an omnipotent agent. Still, as long as I believe myself to be an individual, I will believe that I make choices.

Or we could put it the other way around. One might say, in effect: *I believe I choose, therefore I believe I am.*

The web of causes and conditions that shapes any particular choice or decision has no beginning, no ultimate ground or point of origin. In Buddhist jargon, a choice is "dependently originated." In the context of first-person experience, the groundlessness of choices and decisions is immediately evident in the way they manifest spontaneously, without any apparent cause whatsoever. Choices and decisions—like all thoughts—simply happen; they "pop into my head" (as we say) out of nowhere, like magic. For example, everyone has had the experience of not being able to decide what to do in some critical situation. I try and try to make up my mind, with no success. At last I quit trying and just give up. Go to sleep, maybe, or think about something else. And miraculously the decision is made!

The truth is that I never know what I will choose or decide until after the fact, for until the choice is actually "made," I can in principle always change my mind and do something different. And even after deciding on one alternative, I may and often do reverse course and go off in an entirely different direction. And this can happen repeatedly. Such indecisiveness is for some of us an altogether common experience.

To put it in terms I've been using here: I do not *make* choices; like everything else about my present experience, they are given to me. Thinking and choosing are in this sense like digestion or the beating of the heart. I do not compel the intestines to absorb food or the heart to beat. Nor can I force these metabolic functions to stop through a sheer act of will. They obey their own laws. Of course the situation is confused by language, which attributes agency more or less arbitrarily. For example, one does not normally say (in English): *I'm beating my heart.* We certainly do not say: *I am shortening my telomeres so that my body will age*. But we do say: *I'm thinking a thought*, and *I'm making a choice*. Such ways of speaking are dictated by sociolinguistic convention; they underlie what Buddhist philosophers refer to as "conventional truth."

That I do not see this—that is, that I imagine myself as an autonomous agent making choices and decisions—is, according to Buddhist teaching, the most basic, subtle form of ignorance. To be ignorant in this way means that I operate out of a spurious sense of personal freedom and control, dominated by constant self-centered grasping that lacks any sense of proportion or measure. Ignorance of this sort is coupled not only with remorseless discontent but also with a pronounced lack of humility, with arrogance and pride—an inflated sense of one's own power that the Greeks called hubris; and it leads, inexorably, to disappointment and ruin. "For possessive desires at once destroy what they desire and are enslaved by what they destroy."[22]

> The knocking ceased suddenly, although the echoes of it were still in the house. He heard the chair drawn back and the door opened. A cold wind rushed up the staircase, and a long loud wail of disappointment and misery from his wife gave him courage to run down to her side, and then to the gate beyond. The street lamp flickering opposite shone on a quiet and deserted road.

The Cottage of Darkness[23]

> All the world's a stage,
> And all the men and women merely players;
> They have their exits and their entrances;
> And one man in his time plays many parts,
> His acts being seven ages.[24]

SAM WAS MY FIRST CHILD. My wife's water broke at home, in the early hours before dawn, fouling the clean sheets where she had been sleeping. This spilling of a mysterious bodily fluid was the first indication that he was on his way. The second sign of his immanent arrival was pain. The contractions began in the car on the way to the hospital, and they continued for the next eight hours in cycles tracked on a machine set up next to my wife's hospital bed. Every time I watched the needle rise into its slow sweep across the backlit screen, I knew what was coming. Within moments, the first flicker of tension would appear on her face; that tiny compression of the lips, the narrowing of the eyes that signaled the beginning of yet another round of excruciating pain. Over the hours that followed, Sam's entrance into this world was accompanied by a cataract of sweat, mucus, blood, and tears. The birth of a human being is, by and large, a messy, agonizing business.

If it's this difficult for the mother, one can only imagine how traumatic it must be for the fetus. I mean this literally: one can *only* imagine.

The ability to remember is linked to language acquisition. Most of us vaguely recall a few events that can be reliably dated back to around age three, but memory simply does not stretch back far enough to encompass the primordial event of our physical birth. Still, we know this much: when the amniotic sac ruptures, a tiny person is forcefully ejected from the dark, fluid warmth of the uterus into the brash light of the outside world with all its noise and confusion, its sharp angles and rough, dry surfaces. By the time my son emerged from the narrow passage of the cervix, the pressure had literally deformed his skull, compressing the soft bone into an elongated cylinder. His eyes were squeezed shut, his lips pursed, his tiny fists clenched. He gulped at the hostile air like some alien creature hauled up from the ocean's depths. Thankfully, within a few hours his head returned to its original shape, but the ordeal of birth must have left a more enduring mark on his delicate psyche.

> At first the infant,
> Mewling and puking in the nurse's arms.[25]

One could say that the story of the self actually begins nine months earlier, at conception. And for all we know it begins even earlier than that. Objective memory extends back only so far; the probing eye of science a bit further; beyond that, we encounter an immense diversity of culturally instantiated beliefs in a life previous to this one. The Indian Buddhist tradition adopted from the Upanishads a doctrine of reincarnation that suggests one's present life is only the most recent in an infinite series. Similar beliefs can be found among the ancient Greeks, Neoplatonic Roman philosophers, gnostic Christians, and Celtic pagans. Contemporary Hasidic Jews find justification for belief in rebirth both in the Kabbalah and in the Hebrew Bible. For example, Jeremiah 1:4–5 reads: "The word of the Lord came to me, saying, 'Before I formed you in the womb I knew you, before you were born I set you apart; I appointed you as a prophet to the nations." And again, in Psalm 139:15–16: "My frame was not hidden from you when I was made in the secret place, when I was woven together in the depths of the earth. Your eyes saw my unformed body; all the days ordained for me were written in your book before one of them came to be."

Writing for the *New York Times*, the philosopher Susan Schneider—an authority on artificial intelligence—informs us that "the nature of the self is a matter of intense philosophical controversy."[26] Which is to say, in this arena one is free to believe or not believe pretty much anything. Nevertheless, though I may believe in a life before this one, and another life before that, belief in reincarnation offers no clue as to where this succession of past lives finds its ultimate source. Whether articulated as a tenet of religious faith or as an airtight conclusion to a reasoned argument, beliefs and convictions about the nature of the self and its origins are eventually swept up in the flood of human experience, a mighty river of life that bubbles up from the darkness of a hidden spring. Marilynne Robinson identifies this hidden spring, the source of our individuality, as "the great given of existence":

> I am hungry, I am comfortable, I am a singer, I am a cook. The abrupt descent into particularity in every statement of this kind, Being itself made an auxiliary to some momentary accident of being, may only startle in the dark of the night, when the intuition comes that there is no proportion between the great given of existence and the narrow vessel of circumstance into which it is inevitably forced. "I am Ozymandias, king of kings. Look upon my works, ye mighty, and despair."[27]

The darkness at the deepest interiority of this "narrow vessel of circumstance" is, strictly speaking, neither a something nor a nothing, and for this reason it cannot be appropriated either as a claim to knowledge or even as the subject of a belief. On the contrary, this darkness is made accessible to us only in our most vulnerable moments, as an intuition, or perhaps a startling revelation, of the evanescence and fragility of the individual self, this "king of kings" whose existence is, after all, nothing but a tiny wave momentarily cresting on the surface of an ocean whose depths we cannot begin to fathom. Such an intuition may be facilitated by language and thought, memory and imagination, but has ultimately to do with a realm where the mind finds no purchase and all the casual certainties of knowledge and belief are expunged. What I mean by darkness is, then, a not knowing of what cannot, by its nature, be known, if by "knowing" we mean to objectify, understand, or explain in any literal sense. It is simply not possible to approach the darkness at the core of the self as a mystery to be explained away. Explanation is necessarily entangled with the particular, and a particular "thing" is precisely what this darkness at our core—the mystery of Being—is *not*.[28]

When we speak of darkness in this way, we necessarily abandon referential language and enter the realm of metaphor. The language of the literal—of empirical science and reason—is unable to engage with this mysterious darkness because whatever is subject to objective definition—what can be reduced to its parts, analyzed, classified, and placed in a systematic taxonomy where "this" opposes "that"—is to that very extent no longer the sheer, inexplicable wonder of Being. To encounter the darkness at the interior of the self is, as J. D. Salinger put it, "to be with God before He said, Let there be light"—that is, before there is either light or darkness in any literal sense.[29]

In any case, literal darkness is not the living, breathing darkness that lies at the core of the self. This insight is concisely embodied in the Sanskrit *maya*, a word that simultaneously denotes both "measurement"—the division of lived, experiential reality into units of time and space—and "illusion," suggesting that what can be measured or demarcated is by definition only superficially true or real. To measure, define, or classify is to focus attention on the particularity of the wave rather than on the sea from which it rises and to which it returns, on the individual rather than on the darkness at its core.

To be somebody—to have an individual identity, a personality—is to have emerged out of the depths of a darkness that cannot be objectified and to carry within oneself the impenetrable stamp of that same darkness. Darkness is our inescapable, private truth, a secret buried deep at the center of a self otherwise defined by its endless pretensions to know and, where it does not and cannot know, its endless thirst to believe. But the dark interior of the self cannot be grasped through knowledge or belief.

When it comes to having an identity, what I am not—what cannot be objectified—is evidently every bit as important as what I am.

According to the developmental psychologist Jean Piaget, a newborn infant makes no clear distinction between itself and others. There is only a wordless, undivided *this*, an all-inclusive, pure, unbroken sense of unity and presence that Freud—borrowing a phrase coined by the French writer Romain Rollard—referred to dismissively as "the oceanic feeling." Piaget argued that this primitive developmental stage, which he called "indissociation," precedes the formation of the ego and is manifest above all with the infant's sense of unfettered peace while feeding at the mother's breast, a feeling that itself replicates the earlier security of the womb. The individual self is, then, initially experienced by the infant as an inchoate sense of loss triggered, first, by expulsion from the womb and then repeatedly as separation from the breast.

From the psychologist's point of view, it makes sense to confine one's interest to the formation of the ego or personality as a developmental process unfolding after the birth of the infant, but my existence as an individual—this narrow vessel of circumstance—may well have its roots in deeper soil. As I mentioned above, this sense of loss may go back in some form to the moment of conception, or—if you are inclined to believe in reincarnation—before that. What is important, however, is not when or why, or even how, this experience of loss occurs, but rather where it is located: namely, in the very structure of the personality, as its defining characteristic. The experience of loss is inextricably embedded in the individual's sense of itself as one person distinct from others; it abides there as a remnant of the unfathomable darkness of Being out of which the momentary accident of being emerges. Although the self is defined by a sense of loss, precisely what has been lost remains—from the perspective of the individual—always and forever unknown. It is the primal loss of not knowing who I am, of not being *able* to know who I am.

Over time the infant comes to identify with this sense of loss and—in a massive act of defiance—to interpret her growing self-awareness as a source of agency and power. This process dramatically accelerates with the acquisition of language. To truly separate oneself from other people and from the world of objects "out there," the infant must learn not only to speak and remember but also to say *no*. From the developmental point of view, this single syllable is the linchpin around which all the more elaborate linguistic and conceptual distinctions turn; it is a seamless verbal fortification, a moat encircling the citadel of the self, a protective barrier interposed between the child and its world. From this seed issues a binary conceptual scheme that proliferates into reified ideas of me and not me, mine and yours, right and wrong, truth and error, reality and illusion, all linked to emotions of greed and aversion, desire and fear. *No* is our interior darkness made visible and stripped of all mystery. *No* is nobody become somebody, the unknowable magically transformed by language into a distinct individual self surrounded by an infinity of particular "things" that can be held at bay, classified, and evaluated. Through the power of this word the inchoate sense of loss at the root of the developing personality is increasingly circumscribed by language and so brought under nominal control by the toddler, who learns to conceive of herself as an agent, an actor with a will of her own around which the external world takes shape.

With the development of linguistic competence, the child becomes conscious of and subject to the views of adult others who wield words and ideas that define the self with ever greater precision, as male or female, clever or dull, attractive or plain, good at this and bad at that. I vividly recall, in this context, an exchange that transpired between my then two-year-old son and his mother. Apropos of nothing in particular, my wife had exclaimed, "Oh Sammy, you're just so handsome!" He looked up at her for a moment with an expression that suggested dour consternation, then replied: *Sammy not hansome. Sammy not ugy. Sammy just Sammy.* It's worth noting that at this developmental stage he still referred to himself in the third person, as if this person "Sammy" was hovering out there in the world, two or three steps removed, an identity still waiting to be claimed—or not. It's interesting, as well, that whatever reluctance my son may have felt at the time about claiming "Sammy" as his own, he nevertheless had no compunction about defending Sammy from what he obviously perceived as an unwelcome violation of Sammy's space—a further narrowing of the definition of Sammy's identity, and so, an increasing sense of confinement and, therefore, of discomfiting loss.

Nevertheless, the name our parents give us eventually becomes our own, and what began as an experience of inchoate loss gradually evolves into a fixed persona that has to be defended against the threat of all those other people and things that are not me. Happiness means getting what *I* want, and what *I* want, above all, is both to protect myself from the encroachment of others and simultaneously to have those others reaffirm my own importance by constantly directing their attention toward me. Every parent is familiar with this mindset and the associated behaviors, which can be either charming or, on a bad day, tiresome and annoying. In any case, the two desires, to push away and to draw in, are enmeshed, so the more the child wins at this game, the more she reinforces the sense of isolation at their center, until at last the self is sharply delineated as a unique individual quite securely imprisoned in a fortress of solitude.

To be precise, it is not that the individual is locked inside a prison; rather the individual simply *is* the prison. When I conceive of myself as a distinct "somebody," I take this prison—this cottage of darkness—not simply as my place of residence but as my *self*. Buddhism has traditionally maintained that the sense of being imprisoned by or in the self is the source of a deep and pervasive existential anxiety that permeates human experience at every level. Life as an individual is a continuous struggle made manifest in the ceaseless interpersonal conflict and societal unrest that has defined human history for as far back as memory reaches. In the West, the story of how this comes to be—what is lost in the process of becoming somebody—is inscribed in Genesis, the opening book of the Hebrew Bible.

We all know the story. Adam and Eve find themselves living in a newly created world, naked and blameless, until sampling the fruit of the Tree of the Knowledge of Good and Evil—about which they had been warned by their loving but stern father, who vainly strove to protect their innocence, just as the prince's father, the king of the Shakyas, strove to preserve Gautama's innocence by keeping him locked in the palace. Immediately after eating they become ashamed of their nakedness, and in this newly acquired self-consciousness, they cover themselves with fig leaves. When God discovers them, his first question is, *Who told you that you were naked?* There can be only one answer: a voice in their heads, the voice of a conscience that did not exist until they ate of the fruit. And now this voice divides everything into two fundamental categories: me and not me, what is acceptable and what is not. God the Father must know what it means to have a conscience; it was precisely what he wanted to protect them from. In the context of the Genesis story, it's difficult not to see God's ambiguous presence—the presence of the omniscient, omnipotent adult—as the source of this taint of judgment that infects the children, the "original sin" of the self-conscious individual.

I am aware that to cast God in this unfavorable light is to introduce a difficult and unorthodox problem of theodicy. Be that as it may, as parents we cherish our children's innocence, but at the same time it is we—the adults—who teach them what it means to be isolated and ashamed. We are the masters of language and binary thought from whom they learn how to say "no," how to deploy the first-person pronoun, how to judge and choose and express preferences by putting labels on everything. We provide a model of what it means to have a particular self built upon ideas of right and wrong, likes and dislikes, fears and desires. We do all of this because, as adults, we can't imagine how to do—how to *be*—anything or anyone else. For the child, what inevitably follows is both the seductive power and the curse of life as a self-conscious individual, the wicked irony of an initial sense of loss ennobled and glorified beyond recognition. To be somebody—to have a personality, an identity—is to attempt to escape the original sense of loss by projecting it outward into the ever-present, ambiguous threat of a world simultaneously dreaded and craved. This world outside the self—a concretized, externalized darkness—includes, oddly enough, my body as well as the bodies of others, and so not only youth and beauty but also old age, sickness, and death.

None of this can be avoided. It is, at any rate, given, whether as the original sin of Christianity or as Buddhism's primordial ignorance. This is simply where I find myself—ejected from the garden, or the palace, immersed in existential anxiety and forced to till the earth from which I came and to which I shall return. Behold, I am no longer an innocent child. I have grown up to be a discrete individual with an identity shaped by views and opinions, predilections, aesthetic tastes, beliefs and convictions and a myriad of other incidentals peculiar to my circumstances in life.

I express my individuality through a constantly shifting panorama of masks. Shakespeare counts seven, but the figure is arbitrary; there are many more than seven roles we are compelled to play in this majestic theater. I am for some time a child, then a student, *the whining schoolboy, with his satchel / And shining morning face, creeping like snail / Unwillingly to school.* Later still I am a lover, a husband, an adult who must go to work, earn a living by the sweat of my brow, pay the bills. And then, inevitably, I am an old man clothed in *lean and slipper'd pantaloon / With spectacles on nose and pouch on side.* This grand drama of being somebody is sustained by continually focusing attention on the voices in my head, by obsessing over my body and its needs, by incessantly thinking about how I appear in the eyes of others, measuring myself by the standards of the world outside. All of which serves to occlude the whisper of an aboriginal darkness that sounds through (*personare*) the shifting masks of the personality.

Who am I, really?

Nothing about the physical self remains unchanged—even brain cells undergo constant transformation as we age. Nor is there any element of our first-person experience that remains the same over time: memories morph like clouds in the sky, as the years pass the oldest among them dissipate while new ones are constantly being framed, colored by a shifting mélange of hopes and dreams. What consumed my attention yesterday is forgotten today, replaced by some new passion. In English we talk about "my body" and "my memories"—as if this particular body and these particular memories were mere possessions, trappings that could be stripped away from a solid, unchanging core, leaving that core—"me"—entirely devoid of any particular features. But then, we also routinely use the reflexive pronoun *my*self—as if even the core self were an extraneous possession of an even deeper self—the self out of which, perhaps, my two-year-old son was speaking when he referred to "Sammy" in the third person. All of this is taken for granted in the way we as adults think and speak, a way of thinking and speaking that leads, inevitably, to the postulation of an infinite regression of "core selves." Only a very few—the philosophers and contemplatives—make it their business to notice the ontological presuppositions built into English grammar, how the illusion of an unchanging, individual self is fabricated by language and binary, conceptual thought.

Biologists, however, take all of this for granted in their professional life—it's simply built into the scientific paradigm that governs their work—which is why they speak not of an unchanging individual but rather of an *organism* composed of trillions of cells engaged in an infinitely complex and harmonious dance. The Czech immunologist Miroslav Holub writes: "What is known as the death of an individual and defined as the stoppage of the heart—or, more accurately, as the loss of brain functions—is not, however, the death of the system that guards and assures its individuality."[30] His reflections were prompted by the discovery of a muskrat that had fallen into his empty swimming pool and been shot by a neighbor who attacked the unfortunate creature with a shotgun, blasting away "until all that was left was a shapeless, soggy ball of fur with webbed hind feet and bared teeth." Holub describes how he disposed of the carcass and, while cleaning up the mess, indulged in an extended reflection on the microscopic components of the so-called muskrat: red and white blood cells, adrenaline and corticotropin, endorphins, denaturing proteins and disintegrating peptide chains—all of them now splattered across the concrete. "Bewildered by the unusual temperature and salt concentration, lacking unified signals and the familiar gentle ripples of the vascular endothelium, they were nonetheless alive and searching for whatever they were destined to search for . . . In spite of the escalating losses, these huge home-defense battalions were still protecting the muskrat from the sand, cement, lime, cotton grass; they recognized, reacted, signaled, immobilized, died to the last unknown soldier in the last battle beneath the banner of an identity already buried under the spruces."

For a biologist, the word *muskrat* is nothing more than a convenient fiction, a label pasted over an organized system of parts, each of which is in its turn infinitely divisible. Ultimately the whole reductionist notion of "parts" gives way to the subatomic realm of quantum mechanics, a mereological world where it no longer makes sense to speak of objective truth or reality. This is a world where the very distinction between subject and object, observer and observed, collapses in on itself like a dying star.

But there's no need to invoke the arcane concepts of mereology and quantum mechanics in order to illustrate the way language masks the fundamentally ungraspable nature of the self. That a word may under certain circumstances function as a convenient fiction is a commonly recognized linguistic phenomenon. For example, in the sentence "It was raining yesterday, but today it is snowing" there is no implied subject or agent to which the *it* refers. We might more accurately say, "Yesterday rain was falling, but today snow is falling"—which is exactly what some languages (such as Hindi, Chinese, and Turkish) do. When an English speaker says, "It is raining," the word *it* functions as what linguists call a "dummy pronoun"—that is, a pronoun that has no referent but is syntactically required in order for the sentence to convey meaning. From the Buddhist perspective, the first-person pronoun *I* functions in exactly this way.

Nevertheless, to be somebody is to think of oneself as an independent, unchanging monad that moves through life adopting and then shedding one identity after another, from the innocence of early childhood to the resolute self-consciousness of the adult, to illness, infirmity, and old age. To be somebody is, inevitably, to look up one day and see a new, barely recognizable face in the mirror, a face diminished by the passing of time, dissolving back into the darkness from which it emerged.

> Last scene of all,
> That ends this strange eventful history,
> Is second childishness and mere oblivion,
> Sans teeth, sans eyes, sans taste, sans everything.[31]

Under the circumstances it is tempting to say of the individual self, with deference to the Greek philosopher Parmenides, *ex nihilo nihil fit*: out of nothing comes nothing. A nothing that only seems to be born and to die. But to be an individual self is far from nothing. To be an individual among others is what makes life interesting and fulfilling. The ego is, admittedly, essential to the things we most value in life, to accomplishments in the sciences, the arts, and many other arenas, which are driven at least in part by the desire for recognition, the self-centered urge to be seen and acknowledged. It is, I would go so far as to say, impossible to imagine life on any other terms than those set by the ego.

Self-inquiry may begin with speculation and rational analysis, but useful as they are, the discursive activities of the mind merely skim the surface of our inner life. Ironically, analytic thinking can actually amplify the self's false sense of agency, offering, as it does, the promise of some abstract, transcendent truth that can be fixed in thought. In matters of the spirit, reason is therefore of limited and—if its limitations are not clearly understood—dubious value. The inspiration to dig deeper than words and ideas must be triggered by an existential crisis of the sort invoked by Marilynne Robinson in the quotation early in this chapter, a startling and ultimately painful intuition that cuts through all our formidable cognitive and emotional defenses. Nisargadatta Maharaj, the great twentieth-century teacher of Vedanta, once told a visitor to his tiny apartment in Bombay, "If you have no problem of suffering and release from suffering, you will not find the energy and persistence needed for self-enquiry. You cannot manufacture a crisis. It must be genuine."

"How does a genuine crisis happen?"

"It happens every moment, but you are not alert enough. A shadow on your neighbor's face, the immense and all-pervading sorrow of existence is a constant factor in your life, but you refuse to take notice. You suffer and see others suffer, but you don't respond."[32]

The initial crisis, and the painful intuition it generates, manifest in a heartfelt, anguished response to the suffering of Ozymandius, which is to say, a response to the ceaseless toil of the isolated individual, impotently striving to build an empire that cannot be vanquished by the shifting sands of time. Ozymandius is, of course, all of us; our response to his predicament is a response to our own. And so this crisis that Nisargadatta speaks of, and the accompanying anguish, is infused with humility and, as it matures, with awe and reverence for what is beyond our comprehension: the cottage of darkness where the king of kings makes his real home. As Wendell Berry has written, "Reverence gives standing to creatures, and to our perception of them, just as the law gives standing to a citizen. Certain things appear only in certain lights."[33] And so it is. Only in the reverential light cast by the flames of love and grief are we able to perceive clearly what we can never know, and so give standing to the miracle at the root of our existence here, together, as narrow vessels of circumstance adrift on a sea of dreams.

Absence and Presence

> In the beginning God created the heavens and the earth. And the earth was without form, and void; and darkness was on the face of the deep. And the Spirit of God was hovering over the face of the waters.

SO OPENS THE ACCOUNT of creation in the King James Bible, a poetic evocation of the obscure relationship between absence and presence, nothing and everything. This is difficult, slippery territory. In working to understand the nature of this relationship, we are drawn ever deeper into the cottage of darkness to the very limits of language and conceptual thought.

The Hebrew word *tohu*—here translated as "without form"—occurs nineteen times in the Bible, rendered in varying contexts as wasteland, wilderness, an empty place, nothingness, vanity, and confusion. *Bohu* ("void") appears only three times: once in Genesis 1:2 (above), once again in Isaiah 34:11 (there translated as "emptiness"), and a third time in Jeremiah 4:23, in direct reference to Genesis and so preserving the translation as "void." These are rarely used, fearful words, and they are meant to be fearful. According to a note in the Oxford Annotated Bible, the formless void that somehow precedes or underlies creation is associated with an ancient belief that the world originated from "a watery chaos, personified as a dragon in the Babylonian creation epic." This "dragon" is the Leviathan referred to in Job and the Psalms, a fire-spitting, serpentine creature with fangs and claws—a graphic embodiment of our primal terror in the face of an abyss of nothingness undefined by time or space, an impenetrable, ungraspable, fathomless black hole: the black hole out of which we emerge and into which we fear our inevitable return. The early Hebrews were not predisposed to philosophical or speculative thought, but this ancient story of the universe emerging *ex nihilo* resonates with a mythopoetic authority that has captivated the imagination of generations of commentators who struggled to come to terms with their own fears of what cannot, by its nature, be known.

Like his Hebrew predecessors, the Greek philosopher Aristotle (384–322 BCE) found any reference to absolute nothingness troubling. For Aristotle, the problem was not so much poetic or psychological as rational. In his *Physics* he maintained that matter could have no beginning, so the world must have existed from eternity. In Aristotle's view, a beginning would itself have to begin, and that second beginning would in turn have to begin, implying an infinite regress and therefore a logical fallacy. One might wonder what exactly is the difference between an endless regress of beginnings and no beginning at all. Nevertheless, marking, as he did, the commencement of what would become the long tradition of Western reason, Aristotle's opinion was enormously influential and more or less prevailed for centuries, even though it clearly rejected the biblical account of the creation. The Alexandrian Christian John Philoponus (490–570 CE) offered a series of ad hoc arguments against Aristotle's position, but another three centuries would pass before Sa'adiah ben Yosef Gaon (882–942)—a Jewish theologian writing in Arabic—composed his masterwork, *The Book of Beliefs and Opinions*, in which he countered Aristotle's fear of infinite regress with a rigorous, systematic defense of the idea of creation from nothing. Over time, his arguments were refined by other Muslim scholars, who carried them across the Middle East into North Africa and from there into Moorish Spain, where they caught the attention of the twelfth-century Sephardic philosopher Maimonides. Maimonides drew on them in his efforts to harmonize Aristotelian reason with the teachings of the Bible. This project had already led him to study of the *Sefer Yetzi-*

rah, a text that had engaged the attention of Sa'adiah Gaon, as well. The *Sefer Yetzirah* is, so far as we know, the first place the Hebrew expression *yesh me-ayin* ("something from nothing") appears in print. In referring to God as the creator, the second chapter of this work contains the line "He made His *ayin yesh*," which is generally understood to mean "He made that which wasn't into that which is," or—more provocatively—"He made His nothingness into something." Later Kabbalistic authors went so far as to assert that *ayin* ("nothingness") is another name for God, in this way linking the infinite and the void as two aspects of the divine. Carried forward by Jewish philosopher-mystics and Christian apophatic theologians, the doctrine of creation from nothing increasingly gained prestige until, at long last, it became respectable for Christian intellectuals to conceive of a nothing out of which everything is born. In 1215, at the fourth Lateran Council, Pope Innocent III certified *creatio ex nihilo* as the official doctrine of the Roman Catholic Church. After a thousand years the conflict between Aristotle and the Leviathan was resolved. The serpent prevailed.

Behind all of these developments looms the figure of Sa'adiah ben Yosef Gaon, an enormously original thinker. But even the most creative mind does not operate in a cultural vacuum. Where did he derive the inspiration for his radically new understanding of the relationship between absence and presence? And how is it that his ideas gained so much traction among European intellectuals, both Jewish and Christian? There may well be no single answer to these questions, but history provides some tantalizing clues.

Rabbi Sa'adiah Gaon was born in Egypt, but he lived and worked for eleven years in Baghdad under the Abbasid Caliphate, during what is often considered the Golden Age of Islam. Arabs had conquered Persia in 651 CE, incorporating it into a vast Islamic empire that stretched from Spain to the frontiers of South Asia. Persian bureaucrats were employed as officials in the territorial government, and Persian culture was viewed with favor by the ruling elite of Baghdad. During the seventh and eighth centuries, foreign ideas flowing west out of India into Persia exerted a profound influence on Muslim intellectuals, who in turn passed these ideas along to Europe. Among them was the ten-digit Indian numerical system, incorporating the concept of a number that is, in itself, nothing. This system was described in 825 CE by the Persian mathematician Muhammad Ibn Musa al-Khwarizmi (ca. 780–850) in a work synthesizing Greek and Indian thought. The Sanskrit name for this mysterious number was *shunya*. The phonetically similar Arabic word *sifr* ("empty") was adopted as a translation for Sanskrit *shunya*, which was represented by a small, open circle. By the early ninth century the Moors had conquered Spain and Sicily, bringing with them this revolutionary mathematical concept; al-Khwarizmi's book was translated into Latin in 1145 (seventy years before the fourth Lateran Council met in Rome) and was, for the next four centuries, the principal mathematical textbook in European universities (the English word *algorithm* is derived from his name). In Italy *sifr* became *zefiro*, *zefro*, or *zevero*, corresponding to the French *zéro*, which—minus the accent—made its way into English.

Sa'adiah Gaon was born some thirty years after al-Khwarismi's death. Though he does not appear to have directly referred in his writing to the concept of zero, it is difficult to believe he would not have been familiar with al-Khwarizmi's work. In any case, Sa'adiah Gaon's defense of creation *ex nihilo* and al-Khwarizmi's explication of the mathematical concept of zero moved together from Persia through the Middle East, across North Africa and into Moorish Spain, where both were simultaneously diffused into European culture.

Zero is the symbol for a number that is at once both nothing and something. In his book *The Nothing That Is: A Natural History of Zero*, Robert Kaplan nicely captures the paradoxical nature of zero: "Names belong to things, but zero belongs to nothing. It counts the totality of what isn't there."[34]

Zero as a placeholder—used, for example, in a base ten system to mark the difference between one (1) and ten (10)—was common in the ancient world. But for the ancients a placeholder was not itself a number. Numbers have computational properties; they are used to count things. Numbers don't apply where there's nothing to count. All of this was turned on its head by Indian mathematicians, who conceived, for the first time, of zero as having computational properties, though admittedly unlike the properties of any other number. First of all, addition and subtraction with zero changes nothing: add zero to any number—including itself—and the sum is that same number; subtract zero from any number and once again the number remains unchanged. But multiplication and division yield even more startling results. Multiply any number by zero and the product is zero; divide by zero and no matter what the dividend the quotient is *infinity*—which mathematicians still regard not as a number but rather as an exceedingly odd "concept." As Charles Seife writes in *Zero: The Biography of a Dangerous Idea*, "Zero is powerful because it is infinity's twin. They are equal and opposite, yin and yang. They are equally paradoxical and troubling."[35] In other words, zero is where nothing meets and mingles not just with some particular thing but with *everything*. As a mathematical concept, zero locates the interface between absence and presence, and in this respect it defies the law of noncontradiction, which states that contradictory propositions cannot both be true in the same sense at the same time. Considered to be one of the "laws of thought" and a cornerstone of reason, the law of noncontradiction finds its classical source in Aristotle's metaphysics. And so, as Seife has it, "Zero conflicted with the fundamental philosophical beliefs of the West, for contained within zero are two ideas that were poisonous to Western doctrine. Indeed, these concepts would eventually destroy Aristotelian philosophy after its long reign. These dangerous ideas were the void and the infinite."[36]

No one knows exactly where the idea of "zero" as a placeholder first emerged; it appears to have been the common property of widely dispersed ancient civilizations. But historians agree that regardless of where it originated, India was where zero was transformed from mere placeholder to a legitimate number in its own right. And it was this transformation—a prodigious feat of imagination—that gave zero its mysterious power to absorb and defy all contradictions.

The earliest known reference to mathematical zero appears in the *Chandah Shastra*, a text on Sanskrit prosody attributed to an otherwise unknown author named Pingala and dated to sometime in the first few centuries BCE. The text unfortunately does not include any example of symbolic notation, but Pingala explicitly uses the Sanskrit word *shunya* to refer to the result of subtracting a number from itself. The oldest recorded use of symbolic notation for zero as a number has now been traced back through radiocarbon dating to as early as the third century CE; hundreds of examples have been found in a birchbark text known as the Bakhshali manuscript, which seems to have been intended for use by merchants as a practical manual on arithmetic. Here zero is indicated by a solid dot. By the fourth century the same word *shunya* appears in another text, the *Aryabhatiya*, in the context of a fully developed system of decimal place-value notation. A century later the mathematician Bhaskara, in a commentary on the *Aryabhatiya*, used a circle to represent *shunya*, which is the earliest recorded instance of the notation that has now become virtually universal. At that time, however, the circle was perhaps not yet standardized, since a mathematician by the name of Brahmagupta, a contemporary of Bhaskara, used the same solid dot that occurs in the Bakhshali manuscript. In his *Brahmasputha Siddhanta*, composed around 650 CE, Brahmagupta referred to the dot as *shunya* or, alternatively, *kha*—a cavity, hollow, or empty space, and by extension, the Sanskrit word for "sky." Nevertheless, the use of *shunya* seems at this point to have become more or less fixed. Brahmagupta's treatise is unprecedented, however, in its meticulous analysis of zero in the context of negative numbers and corresponding algebraic operations. His work leaves no question that by the seventh century, Indian mathematicians had fully conceptualized the role of mathematical zero in the sense familiar to us now.

As it happens, however, this is only half the story of zero's Indian history. In ancient India, zero was not only a mathematical concept.

The Sanskrit word *shunya* is routinely used in Mahayana Buddhist texts dating back to the first few centuries BCE; which is to say, its appearance both as a revolutionary mathematical term and as the expression of a profound, intuitive understanding of the nature of reality—the mark of "transcendent, liberating wisdom" (*prajna-paramita*)—seems to have occurred simultaneously in India. The paradoxical characteristic of mathematical zero—as a nothing that is not only something, but everything—features in the Buddhist notion of *shunya*, but its implications are no longer merely abstract or computational. In the scriptures on perfect wisdom, *shunya* is presented as a fundamental truth of all existence, a truth fully appreciated by spiritual beings known as bodhisattvas, who have achieved this profound insight only as the result of long study and contemplative practice. The famous *Heart Sutra* opens by telling us that the bodhisattva Avalokiteshvara, "moving in the stream of perfect wisdom," looked down over the world and saw that "zero-ness" (*shunya-ta*) is the essential nature of every element of experience—everything that makes up our mental and physical reality:

> Here . . . form is zero-ness and zero-ness itself is form; zero-ness does not differ from form, form does not differ from zero-ness. Whatever is form, that is zero-ness; whatever is zero-ness, that is form. The same is true of feelings, perceptions, impulses, and consciousness.[37]

Nor is the ancient notion of zero as a placeholder marginalized in this literature. In the scriptures on perfect wisdom, this characteristic of zero is an integral component of its status as both absence and presence, simultaneously. To say that every element of experience—every *dharma*—is zero is to say that, like zero, the appearance of individual, self-sufficient things is nothing more than appearance; there is no actual "thing," no individual physical or mental object that truly exists as it appears. The mental or physical object that seems to exist separately from other such things in fact exists only as a placeholder. Which is to say, the individual exists only in relation to what it is not, and what it is not is literally everything else—an infinitude of other apparently individual things. This is the sense in which dharmas are said to be "devoid of essential nature," which is the same as saying that their essential nature is zero-ness.

And so in the *Perfection of Wisdom in Eight Thousand Lines*—perhaps the oldest surviving text of this genre—we are asked, rhetorically: "To what dharma could I point and say that 'it exists' or 'it doesn't exist'?"[38]

> It is precisely through their essential nature that dharmas are not a thing. Their essential nature is no-nature, and their no-nature is their essential nature. All dharmas have only one characteristic, which is no characteristic at all.[39]

"'All things are no-things,' taught the Tathagata [the Buddha], 'therefore they are things.'"[40] Perfect wisdom, then, is a deep innate understanding that breaks free of our normal habits of thinking and speaking, habits that compel us to both conceive and perceive individual things literally as either existing or not existing, as either this or that. Rather, as seen through the eye of perfect wisdom, things are not things, and not things are things, which means that they only seem to arise and pass away. This is true, according to the *Diamond Sutra*, for living beings as well, who merely appear to be self-contained individuals subject to birth and death: "'Beings, beings' . . . the Tathagata has taught that they are all no-beings. In this way has he spoken of 'all living beings.'"[41] Nothing whatsoever is exempted: "This entire universe the Tathagata has taught as no-universe. In this sense it is called a 'universe.'"[42]

> Therefore, Shariputra, in zero-ness there is no form, nor feeling, nor perception, nor impulse, nor consciousness; no eye, ear, nose, tongue, body, mind; no forms, sounds, smells, tastes, or tactile objects . . . There is no ignorance, no extinction of ignorance . . . no decay and death and no end to decay and death. There is no suffering, no origin, no cessation, no spiritual path. There is no wisdom. There is nothing to attain.[43]

"It is on account of this," explains the *Perfection of Wisdom in Eight Thousand Lines*, "that the Tathagata does not fully know the character of any dharma."[44] What is literal or concrete can be fully known or grasped, its character can—at least in principle—be understood empirically, rationally analyzed and explained; what is metaphorical is "as if," and "as if" can only be intuited.

Consider, in this context, what Robert Kaplan has to say about zero as the interface of nothing and everything:

> [I]t is as if there were a layer behind appearances that had no qualities, but took on the character of its surroundings, accommodating itself to our interpretations, as ambergris acquires and retains fugitive fragrances, giving us perfume. *Shunya* isn't so much vacancy, then, as receptivity, a womb-like hollow ready to swell—and indeed it comes from the root *shvi*, meaning swelling. Its companion *kha* derives from the verb "to dig," and so carries the sense of "hole": something to be filled . . . This is the zero of the counting board: a column already there, but with no counters yet in it. This is the zero of the place-holder notation, having no value itself but giving value by its presence to other numerals. These same qualities belong to the variable, the unknown: a potential which the different circumstances of the equations it lies in will differently realize. The background shift is from counters taking their value from being in different places, to a single, receptive place whose circumstances will reveal its hidden value.[45]

The concept of *shunya* evokes the ambiguous, ungraspable nature of what only appears to be literal, concrete truth or reality. The Indian mathematician Bhaskara acknowledges as much when, in a discussion of mathematical zero, he writes: "The arithmetic of known quantity . . . is founded on that of unknown quantity; and . . . questions to be solved can hardly be understood by any, and not at all by such as have dull apprehensions, without the application of unknown quantity."[46] Perhaps the most eloquent classical passage on this aspect of the zero-ness of things comes from the *Diamond Sutra*:

> A phantom's mask, a shooting star,
> a guttering flame.

A sorcerer's trick, a bubble swept
on a swiftly moving stream.
A flash of lightning among dark clouds.
A drop of dew,
a dream.
So should one view all conditioned things.[47]

In his final book, *Brief Answers to Big Questions*, the eminent physicist Stephen Hawking wrote: "I think the universe was spontaneously created out of nothing," and he asks, therefore, "What role is there for God?"[48] One possible response is that the word God may be used to evoke reverence for the sacred dimension of this very nothing, this zero-ness out of which the universe spontaneously manifests and into which it returns in a timeless, ongoing process of creation and destruction that eludes any attempt at reductive explanation. As the twentieth-century philosopher and mystic Simone Weil puts it:

> Contact with human creatures is given us through the sense of presence. Contact with God is given us through the sense of absence. Compared with this absence, presence becomes more absent than absence.[49]

To use the word *God* in this way is to call upon a metaphorical resonance of zero evidently not accessible to Hawking. In his unreflective commitment to the search for literal, objective truth, he is captivated by a radically different metaphor, a peculiarly modern Western picture of the cosmos as a mindless machine—"an aggregate of mechanistic functions and systems, accidentally arranged out of inherently lifeless and purposeless elements."[50]

Nevertheless, even without the word *God*, this sacred, symbolic dimension of zero not available to Hawking is clearly acknowledged in the Mahayana Buddhist tradition, as it was by the Kabbalists, and by medieval Christian mystics who found in nothingness the key to salvation. In *The Mystical Theology of St. Denis* we read: "In knowing nothing he is made to know beyond understanding."[51] The anonymous author of *The Cloud of Unknowing* offers this advice to anyone seeking to know the origin of things:

> Give up this everywhere and this something, in favor of this nowhere and this nothing. Do not worry if your senses have no knowledge of this nothing: truly, I love it all the better for that. They have no knowledge of it because it is something so noble in itself. This nothing can be better felt than seen, for it is quite obscure and quite dark to those who have only been looking at it for a short time; yet, to put it more accurately, in experiencing it a soul is blinded by abundance of spiritual light more than by darkness or lack of bodily light. Who is it that calls it nothing? It is our outer man, to be sure, not our inner. Our inner man calls it Everything; for from it he learns well to have knowledge of all things, bodily or spiritual, without specific regard to any one thing by itself.[52]

Wisdom, Love, and Grief

He wants only one, most precious thing:
To see, purely and simply, without name,
Without expectations, fears, or hopes,
At the edge where there is no I or not I.[53]

IN 1425, the Italian architect Filippo Brunelleschi provoked a revolution in painting by placing a dot like the dot found in the Bakhshali manuscript in the center of a blank piece of paper. Brunelleschi used this dot as the locus of reference for his drawing of the Baptistry, a famous Florentine building. Although the Greeks appear to have had ways of drawing in perspective, this is the first recorded use of the vanishing point, a zero-dimensional space that marks a location infinitely removed from the viewer. As objects in the drawing fall away into the distance, becoming ever more remote, they simultaneously move ever nearer to the vanishing point. As they do so they become increasingly compacted, eventually melting into the zero-dimensional space at the center of the drawing—an absence that conceals within itself an infinitude of presence.[54] This technique reached an apotheosis with the Dutch architect and engraver Jan Vredeman de Vries, who published his masterwork *Perspective* in 1604–05, which included the sketch below.

The nothing at the center of everything is a nothing that is always already everything, a nothing from which everything overflows and

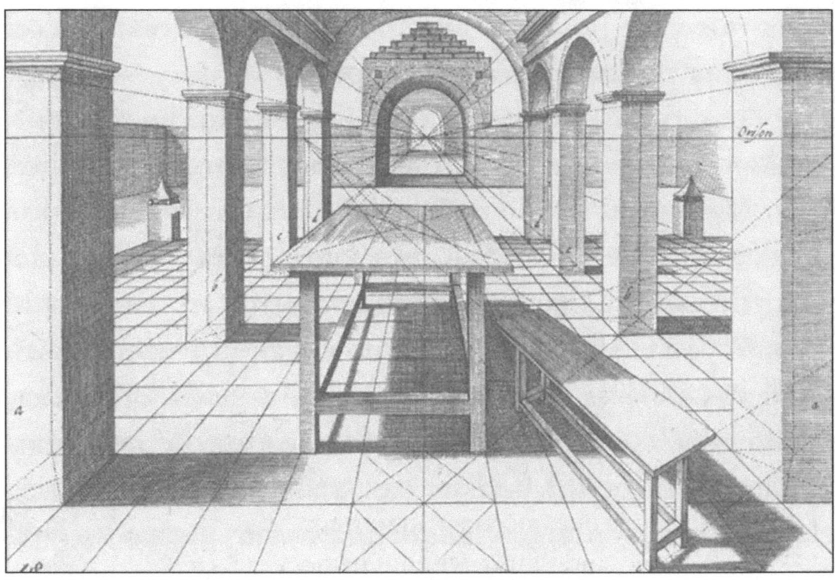

pours forth. This is the wild, incomprehensible miracle of zero as infinity, as the nothingness out of which the universe is spontaneously created. Zero is an absence that points, in its essential nature, beyond itself toward presence, toward the infinite display of apparent things that makes up this universe that is no universe.

But here is yet another mystery of zero-ness: what is *absent* is any particular thing defined in or by itself, as an individual cut off from other similarly distinct individuals; what is *present* is an infinitely complex web of interpenetrating relationships, relationships among individuals who do not exist outside of those relationships. Like the placeholder zero, individuals are nothing in themselves because they exist only in the context of their relations with what they are not. Another way of saying this is that individuals only *appear* to exist as individuals, as zero appears to exist as something rather than nothing. In Mahayana Buddhism merely apparent existence is not presented simply as an abstract mathematical or philosophical concept that bears no relationship to our subjective, inner life. Understanding or "seeing" the merely apparent existence of both the self and its world requires a form of radical introspection that transcends any kind of dualistically structured experience. "Seeing" in this sense is referred to in Tibetan Dzogchen as "the simultaneity of zero-ness and awareness." The Dzogchen scholar David Higgins, citing the fourteenth-century Tibetan visionary Longchen Rabjam, refers to such seeing as "the very wellspring of open awareness that is the vanishing point of mind."[55] When we introduce this perspective—the perspective of the first-person viewer—into Jan Vredeman de Vries's drawing, it becomes immediately apparent that something essential had been left out of the original:[56]

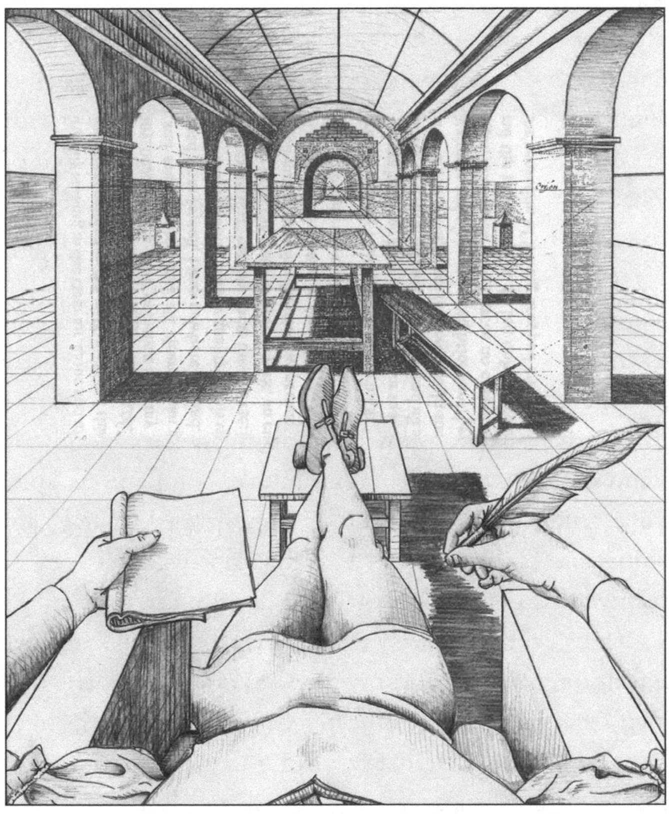

On close examination of the first-person perspective, there appear to be two vanishing points—one "in here" and one "out there"—with the individual and his world suspended between them. The interior vanishing point is a void of pure awareness "beneath" dualistic thoughts and emotions. And so, as accessed on a more intimate level, what I referred to above as "the cottage of darkness" turns out to be illuminated from within by a mysterious, metaphorical light, a mirror-like awareness in which everything is reflected while the mirror remains, in itself, sheer empty space, for it never appears as an object of any kind. One could say that the light of this naturally occurring timeless awareness shining in the deepest region of the self is too bright and clear to be seen, and so is not simply a light hidden in darkness, but a light that *is* darkness—a brilliant darkness, so to speak, seen by seeing nothing, known by knowing nothing.[57]

On the other hand, the exterior vanishing point is seen by seeing everything, known by knowing everything—"without specific regard to any one thing by itself." It is a void encountered when the attention is directed outward toward infinity, a dimensionless abyss out of which pours a profusion of individual objects embracing the entire psychological and physical universe in all its diversity, an immensity of empirically present particulars that includes not only all those other humans who populate my life and the profusion of human artifacts we have crafted through our ingenious machinations, but also all of nature—the earth with its wild luxuriance of lakes and rivers and restless, churning seas, its towering redwoods, its tulips and morning glories, clouds and wind and rain and stars, as well as all our nonhuman companions: spiders and droning bees; our slobbering, precious dogs; grizzly bears; gleaming silver dolphins; and black panthers with their fierce amber eyes.

Oddly, my body is as well an object "out there" in the world, experienced as such by others—a body that is nevertheless, in some peculiarly intimate fashion, my own. But my physical body is not the only thing of "my own" that I experience objectively. From the depths of the first-person vantage point, literally everything that constitutes my private experience of myself as an individual—all my thoughts and feelings and bodily sensations—appear "out there" as possessions or attributes of an assumed core self, the *me* that owns *my* thoughts, *my* feelings, *my* sensations. Of course we can't see these mental objects in the illustration above, but they were undoubtedly present for the artist as he sat contemplating the scene before him—his thoughts and feelings arising and passing away; the sensation of the chair pressing up against his legs, back, and arms; a gentle breeze tickling the hairs on the backs of his hands. Nevertheless—and this is crucial—although the artist is aware of his thoughts and feelings and sensations, he is not, in a similar fashion, aware of the light of awareness in which they appear. That "light" is simply not present to experience in the way that mental and physical objects are present; it is present, rather, in the way the vanishing point is present: as an absence or nothingness that contains everything.

What is perhaps most striking when considering the first-person perspective of the artist is that we can begin to sense how these two vanishing points, one inside and the other outside, only *appear* to be separate, just as zero and infinity appear as nothing and everything but are, in some inexplicable fashion, both separate *and* identical. This hints at

> that mysterious unity that quietly persists amid the spectacle of incessant change: [a] oneness that is everywhere and nowhere, at once in the world and in one's consciousness of it, holding all things together as a coherent totality while also preserving each separate thing in its particularity, and each part of each thing, and each part of that part, and so on ad infinitum.[58]

This unity is mysterious because it is both unified and fragmented. Exploring the farthest reaches of first-person experience, we stumble upon a metaphorical "place" where the discursive mind gives way to an all-embracing brilliant darkness within which, paradoxically, all dualistically structured experience—both the ceaseless activity of the discursive mind and the sensual, physical world—is included or contained. It is as if, through some enigmatic calculus, where I am most myself, in my most extreme subjectivity, is precisely where I cross over the threshold into what I am not. As an individual, I fall through the internal vanishing point of mind only to stream out of the external vanishing point as an infinitude of objectively present "things"—all those others that not only populate my world but are, in some incomprehensible fashion, *within* me so as to constitute my very being, and I am within them. This is a truly profound ecology of mind that intimately and inextricably links each of us not only to other human beings but to the nonhuman world as well.

There is, however, another, even more paradoxical feature of this mysterious, all-embracing light. Although the word *light* is obviously being used metaphorically, such usage appears to stretch the definition of metaphor beyond its capacity to serve. A metaphor is commonly understood as a figure of speech in which a word or phrase is applied to an object to which it is not literally applicable, but in this case there is no object to which the metaphor applies. *Light,* as the word is used here, refers to an empty space that is "known by not knowing" or "seen by not seeing," and is in this peculiar sense a metaphor applied not to a literal object but to what appears to be yet another metaphor. This is language entirely devoid of reference, words unmoored and floating free of referential constraint. Language like this has no fixed meaning to convey; its only concern is with its *effect* on the reader or listener. And the intended effect is to liberate: it is meant to open up the discursive mind to the greater nondual reality in which it subsides.

To relate to all of this not simply as an exotic conceptual game but rather as a living, redemptive truth is referred to in Mahayana Buddhism as *wisdom* (*prajna* or *jnana*): "[a fusing] of the conceptual and experiential in a single experience, the experiential and the conceptual in a single concept."[59] However—to raise a final disconcerting point to which I will return at intervals—it must be acknowledged that the peculiarly modern disjunction between "experience" and "theory" is problematic in this context, based as it is on yet another disjunction between "interior" and "exterior." The idea of the interiority of experience is a product of the imagination rooted in a spatial image drawn from visual perception. It makes perfect sense to speak in literal terms about the inside and outside of physical things that we can see, but to talk about the extreme interiority of the self or mind as the subjective locus for experience of mental (conceptual/theoretical) and physical objects somehow external to it is clearly metaphorical. Strictly speaking, then, Buddhist wisdom cannot be said to be a matter of "experience" as opposed to theory, or to the lived experience *of* some concept. Although as a matter of convenience, we may speak of this intuition of a living, redemptive truth as a melding of the conceptual and the experiential, the radical unknowing that constitutes one of two defining traits of a bodhisattva ultimately defies all such linguistic distinctions. It is not the experience *of* anything in particular, whether that thing is a concept, a theory, or even some inexpressible truth or reality; Buddhist wisdom is found in the silence that engulfs language and thought, a silence that transcends all experience, an empty space out of which experience arises and into which it returns.

Which brings us to the bodhisattva's other defining trait: compassion or love (*karuna*).[60]

In order to get at what is implied by the word *love* in this context, I want to turn for a moment to Tolstoy's famous novella *The Death of Ivan Ilych*. The final chapter has Ivan—a self-assured, confident judge on the Court of Justice—rapidly approaching death:

> From that moment the screaming began that continued for three days, and was so terrible that one could not hear it through two closed doors without horror. At the moment he answered his wife he realized that he was lost, that there was no return, that the end had come, the very end, and his doubts were still unsolved and remained doubts.
>
> "Oh! Oh! Oh!" he cried in various intonations. He had begun by screaming "I won't!" and continued screaming on the letter "o."
>
> For three whole days, during which time did not exist for him, he struggled in that black sack into which he was being thrust by an invisible, resistless force. He struggled as a man condemned to death struggles in the hands of the executioner, knowing that he cannot save himself. And every moment he felt that despite all his efforts he was drawing nearer and nearer to what terrified him. He felt that his agony was due to his being thrust into that black hole and still more to his not being able to get right into it. He was hindered from getting into it by his conviction that his life

> had been a good one. That very justification of his life held him fast and prevented his moving forward, and it caused him most torment of all.[61]

Ivan's fear of the "black sack" is the ancient biblical terror in the face of *tohu-bohu*. It is the fear of the Leviathan, of *shunya-ta*, the abyss of zero-ness, an impenetrable, ungraspable, fathomless breach in the wall of time and space out of which everything emerges and into which everything returns. Ivan's fear is our own primal fear of what grasps us but cannot itself be grasped.

At this point in the story the gestalt abruptly shifts:

> Suddenly some force struck him in the chest and side, making it still harder to breathe, and he fell through the hole and there at the bottom was a light. What had happened to him was like the sensation one sometimes experiences in a railway carriage when one thinks one is going backwards while one is really going forwards and suddenly becomes aware of the real direction.
>
> "Yes, it was not the right thing," he said to himself, "but that's no matter. It can be done. But what is the right thing? he asked himself, and suddenly grew quiet.[62]

Ivan has been struggling for months with a sense of injustice, a conviction that he had lived an upright and moral life and did not deserve this punishment. Struggling, that is, with the conviction that he knew right from wrong, what should and should not be, and what he as an individual deserved, living among others as he had, defined by his role in society. But now his prior certainty vanishes, and he is left with one burning question: how does one live as a man alone, facing death?

> This occurred at the end of the third day, two hours before his death. Just then his schoolboy son had crept softly in and gone up to the bedside. The dying man was still screaming desperately and waving his arms. His hand fell on the boy's

> head, and the boy caught it, pressed it to his lips, and began to cry.
>
> At that very moment Ivan Ilych fell through and caught sight of the light, and it was revealed to him that though his life had not been what it should have been, this could still be rectified. He asked himself, "What *is* the right thing?" and grew still, listening. Then he felt that someone was kissing his hand. He opened his eyes, looked at his son, and felt sorry for him. His wife came up to him and he glanced at her. She was gazing at him open-mouthed, with undried tears on her nose and cheek and a despairing look on her face. He felt sorry for her too.
>
> "Yes, I am making them wretched," he thought. "They are sorry, but it will be better for them when I die." He wished to say this but had not the strength to utter it. "Besides, why speak? I must act," he thought. With a look at his wife he indicated his son and said: "Take him away...sorry for him... sorry for you too...." He tried to add, "forgive me," but said "forego" and waved his hand, knowing that He whose understanding mattered would understand.[63]

Tolstoy has been faulted by some literary critics for his use of theological language in this story. In the view of these critics, expressions like "caught sight of the light" and "He whose understanding mattered" can only indicate that the celebrated author of the humanist classics *War and Peace* and *Anna Karenina* sacrificed artistic integrity for faith—a conclusion that seems to find support in his late-life conversion to the Russian Orthodox Church. In the words of Victor Brombert, Tolstoy's theology appears to these critics as "arbitrary, preachy, painfully lacking in ambiguity and 'levels of meaning.'"[64] Many contemporary Western Buddhists might be inclined to similar thoughts, given Buddhism's historic skepticism toward religious doctrines of a creator God.

But—in my view, at least—it's not that simple. Ivan's revelation in the presence of his wife and son obviously has to do with empathy and compassion, with loving and being loved. Whatever its source, his revelation bears as its fruit love and forgiveness, compassion for himself and for others. In the spirit of the philosopher William James, I propose we tentatively accept that reasonable men and women can disagree on the subject of the origins of such feelings, whether they stem from God or from a weakened liver, or from a liver weakened by God, or from a mind "deranged" by fear and pain. *Ye shall know them by their fruits*. Whatever the source of Ivan's revelation, its fruits are self-evident:

> And suddenly it grew clear to him that what had been oppressing him and would not leave him was all dropping away at once from two sides, from ten sides, and from all sides. He was sorry for them, he must act so as not to hurt them: release them and free himself from these sufferings. "How good and how simple!" he thought. "And the pain?" he asked himself. "What has become of it? Where are you, pain?"
>
> He turned his attention to it.
>
> "Yes, here it is. Well, what of it? Let the pain be."
>
> "And death . . . where is it?"
>
> He sought his former accustomed fear of death and did not find it.
>
> "Where is it? What death?" There was no fear because there was no death.
>
> In place of death there was light.
>
> "So that's what it is!" he suddenly exclaimed aloud. "What joy!"
>
> To him all this happened in a single instant, and the meaning of that instant did not change. For those present his agony continued for another two hours. Something rattled in his throat, his emaciated body twitched, then the gasping and rattle became less and less frequent.
>
> "It is finished!" said someone near him. He heard these words and repeated them in his soul.
>
> "Death is finished," he said to himself. "It is no more!"
>
> He drew in a breath, stopped in the midst of a sigh, stretched out, and died.[65]

What is interesting to me about Tolstoy's novella in the context of this discussion is how much of it ought to be familiar territory for any knowledgeable Buddhist—notwithstanding the theistic language. Ivan is rescued from the terror of the black sack through his discovery of a spontaneously arising capacity for giving and receiving love—a capacity every bit as infinite in reach as the bottomless void it illuminates. In Mahayana Buddhism this capacity for unconditional love is the affective counterpart to wisdom; the difference between the two is only a matter of perspective. Love and wisdom (*karuna* and *prajna*) are, in essence, identical.

Marilynne Robinson writes, "Whoever controls the definition of mind controls the definition of humankind itself, and culture, and history."[66] This is an audacious claim, and it is certainly correct. She makes, as well, the following observation:

> The great breach that separates the modern Western world from its dominant traditions of religion and metaphysics is the prestige of opinion that throws into question the scale of the reality in which the mind participates. Does it open on ultimate truth, at least partially or in momentary glimpses, or is it an extravagance of nature, brilliantly complex yet created and radically constrained by its biology and by cultural influence? Prior to any statement about the mind is an assumption about the nature of the reality of which it is part, and which is in some degree accessible to it as experience or knowledge.[67]

To review the details of this "great breach" would take us far beyond the scope and purpose of this book. But there is no doubt that contemporary intellectual and popular culture in the West is saturated with a materialist picture of the world—a picture rooted in a metaphor of nature as mindless machine—that makes it difficult for us to assimilate an alternative metaphysic. The first step in escaping the grip of this picture, and the metaphor on which it is based, is simply to see that it is, in fact, nothing more than a picture of the world rooted in a metaphor. And it is, moreover, a picture of the world that, in its exclusive valorization of "objectivity," has the effect of blinding us to the vitally important reality of the first-person perspective and the peculiar form of "knowing nothing" or "unknowing" that emerges from the depths of our interiority. Blinding us, that is, to the difference between—to take one obvious example—a secondhand understanding based on my observation of someone else's dying and an understanding of dying based on my first-person experience. Science can tell us a great deal about dying and death from an objective point of view but nothing at all about what it means to directly face one's own imminent demise.

The understanding of the mind that we are exploring here is obviously based on a different picture, and a different metaphor from the one that drives empirical science. From the Mahayana Buddhist point of view, notwithstanding important variations from one tradition to another, there is widespread agreement that at the deepest level of human subjectivity—which is to say, at the deepest level of the mind, deeper than any form of cognitive activity—discursive thought gives way to the luminosity of a pure, contentless awareness. This awareness is in itself both nothing and everything, zero and infinity, an ultimate truth or reality entirely beyond the reach of dualistic experience and therefore beyond any description of the self and the world based on the metaphor of nature as a mindless machine. David Bentley Hart convincingly argues that the metaphysical and spiritual claims that shape the Buddhist picture of the mind are as well the common property of the major theistic faiths, all of which agree especially "on the issue of how divine transcendence should be understood"—namely, as the subjectivity of consciousness, which is "one and indivisible":

> This is not to say that brain states cannot be altered, or that the mind cannot be confused, or that either the operations of the brain or the actions of the mind cannot be multiple. But in order for there to be such a thing as representation, or reason, or conceptual connections, or coherent experience, or subjectivity, or even the experience of confusion, there must

> be a single unified presence of consciousness to itself, a single point of perspective that is, so to speak, a vanishing point, without extension or parts, subsisting in its own simplicity.[68]

As I have been at pains to demonstrate, for Mahayana and Dzogchen Buddhist practitioners, the idea of the fundamental indivisibility of awareness is not simply a metaphysical proposition to be argued for or against. The reflective capacity of the mind—this mysterious "zeroness" without extension or parts—when treated strictly as a concept or logical proposition cannot effectively address the interminable, evidently meaningless suffering of life. "The simultaneity of zero-ness and awareness" functions, rather, as a potent metaphor consistently invoked within the immensity of its boundless associations as a sacred, redemptive truth embodied in the figure of the bodhisattva, a being whose existence as an individual is consciously entangled with the world "out there." Encountered in this way—as a lived truth—it is a metaphor that gives meaning to suffering by making suffering the source of compassion and all-embracing love. With reference to Tolstoy's novella, Brombert suggests that "the final page can stand as an encounter with nothingness or as a metaphor of revelation."[69] Or, we can now safely add, as both an encounter with nothingness *and* a metaphor of revelation. A revelation about, to quote Robinson again, "the scale of the reality in which the mind participates."

The impulse to be seen and accepted, to give and receive love, is the expression of a fervent desire to escape the prison of the individual self. This same desire, manifest in the struggle of the self to be free of itself, is the quintessential religious or spiritual journey. It is a movement not toward the temporary happiness of getting what I want but toward the profound reconciliation with what is given in the course of an ordinary human life. As the paradigm of self-surrender, love will always be an enigma, both desired and feared, for it simultaneously ennobles and erases the individual self. Like dying, love is a surrender to a higher truth—an ultimate reality that is infinitely distant (lying beyond or below thought, reason, perception, and emotion) and yet immediately accessible in the deepest interiority of the self.

That the peculiar power of zero to embody opposites—to be both absent and present, everything and nothing—manifests in the bodhisattva as love is, in one sense at least, not particularly difficult to appreciate, nor is such an idea unique to Buddhism. As the Vedanta teacher Nisargadatta puts it: "Love says 'I am everything.' Wisdom says: 'I am nothing.' Between the two my life flows."[70] I find a similar idea in the following passage from *Thin Places*, a gentle, reflective book by Ann Armbrecht. As a young anthropology student, Armbrecht lived for several years in the remote Nepalese village of Hedangna. Later in life, when she gave birth to a child, she sensed a parallel between the Hedangna peoples' relationship with the land and her own relationship with her infant daughter Avery:

> I thought about mothering and farming the way the villagers farmed in Hedangna. Their intimate connection with the soil allowed them to respond intuitively to it, the way I responded to Avery, anticipating her needs as if they were an extension of my own. This quality of intimacy is accessible not only through mothering, although I came to know it as a mother. It is an intimacy that made porous my own boundaries, seeing that Avery was in me and I in her in ways I could not even begin to understand—a relationship that took time and attention, in which the things that mattered were the things that could not be seen. What does responsibility—the ability to respond—mean, then? What does it take to pause before acting, to remember that the things that seem to be outside, the people and places we love, are also inside, shaping what we see and do in the world? Then limiting our desires is not about denying ourselves, but about coming more deeply into ourselves, as we open to all the selves inside us.
>
> I thought about the different kinds of love, the love of a lover, of romance where the beloved is the star, love where we give and we receive—love that is visible. And there is the quieter, more solitary love of a parent for a child, like growing rice. No shining light. The invisible daily work.[71]

This invisible, daily work, as best I understand it, is the forever unfinished work of a bodhisattva. *Beings are numberless; I vow to save them all.* This work of loving and being loved rescues us from our own inherent nothingness by breaking the individual open to the otherwise hidden presence of all those others who dwell within; at the same time, it makes us forever vulnerable to the suffering of those we love. It is work where the relationship between love and grief is experienced as a sacred, impenetrable mystery, a truth that can only be known through being lived.

There's a parable in Prajnakaramati's commentary on the ninth chapter of Shantideva's *Guide to the Bodhisattva's Way of Life* that illustrates this point. The parable begins with a metaphor. Imagine that all the suffering in the world was compacted into one tiny thread. Now imagine you were to place that thread on your palm, using your thumb to press it down and roll it back and forth. That sensation—of the thread rubbing against your skin—is compared to the way most of us are affected by the suffering of the world. Now imagine that you were to place that same tiny thread underneath your eyelid. That, we are told, is how a bodhisattva experiences the suffering of all sentient beings.

What meaning are we to take from this parable? Why should a "spiritually advanced being" suffer more, not less, than the rest of us? And what does that imply for Buddhist notions of nirvana and awakening? These are hard questions, questions that deserve serious, extended reflection. But for the moment, this much at least is obvious: the love that is equated with wisdom clearly has nothing to do with getting what I want—with "happiness" in any of its customary meanings. Rather such love has to do with how I live with what I'm given. Dostoevsky seems to be expressing something like this in his short story "The Dream of a Ridiculous Man" when he writes: "On our earth we can only love truly by suffering and only through suffering. We can love in no other way and know no other love."[72]

I hear echoes of the Buddhist parable of the thread in these lines as well, from the poet Adrienne Rich:

> The problem is
> to connect, without hysteria, the pain
> of any one's body with the pain of the body's world.[73]

And finally, in the words of Simone Weil:

> In the soul filled by the object no corner is left for saying "I." We cannot imagine such joys when they are absent, thus the incentive for seeking them is lacking.[74]

Just as no one can adequately imagine beforehand what it is to be a parent, so in our present condition we can hardly conceive of a life lived from the understanding that nothing and everything are the same, that darkness and light, goodness and evil, emanate from the same source, and that I am myself a nothing that becomes a something only in relationship with an infinite diversity of others. And yet, until we are able to assimilate some version of these ideas, not just think about them but rather live them as our guiding truth, we cannot appreciate what it might mean to be free of the boundaries that separate us from one another and from the natural world—boundaries that leave each of us isolated and afraid. Assuming Simone Weil is right and we lack the incentive to seek—or even desire—what is utterly beyond our imagining, we can at least wonder. The capacity for wonder is a fundamental attribute of the human spirit, a portal to otherwise inaccessible truths. It is within our power to wonder at the enigmatic figure of the bodhisattva, at the meaning of the word "joy" in a context so closely associated with suffering, at whether this kind of love for one another and for the world—a love so courageous and unreserved—is humanly possible.[75] We can wonder, that is to say, if to experience such uncompromising love and grief is something anyone of us could bear. But here, once again, we may simply have run up against the limits of reason—which is to say, the limits of literal, referential language and all notions of agency, for where the "I" is no longer present, talk of what I might or might not be able to bear is devoid of meaning.

Waking Up

Row, row, row your boat,
gently down the stream.
Merrily, merrily, merrily, merrily,
life is but a dream.

IF LIFE IS NOTHING more substantial than a dream, as this old nursery rhyme suggests—and as Buddhism teaches—then why should we take it seriously? But we do take it seriously. We row not with but against life's current, a current that often seems swift and treacherous. We tug at the oars, struggle and sweat, swerve to avoid rocks and eddies, fearing that at any moment we might capsize and drown—because eventually we will. So this dream of life becomes a nightmare from which we cannot awaken.

According to the ancient legend, after years of searching, the Indian prince Gautama did exactly this—he woke up—and was then known as the Buddha, the "Awakened One." He helped others to do the same and so is recognized as the founder of Buddhism. Over the centuries, as the Indian tradition spread throughout Asia and, more recently, into the West, this experience—the experience of awakening—has retained its place at the center of Buddhist study and practice.

But what does it mean to say that Prince Gautama "woke up"? How can we imagine the unimaginable, that raw, first-person experience? If we cannot imagine, we can at least wonder.

The trope of awakening is predicated on the idea that before he became the Buddha, Gautama was in some sense asleep and dreaming. To speak of awakening in this way is not to suggest that our present life actually *is* a dream, but rather that it's *like* a dream. This simile is at the heart of Buddhism. In fact, we could say that since its first appearance in the Upanishads—a collection of Sanskrit texts that predate Buddhism by centuries—the conviction that birth and death are an illusion (*maya*) has served as the pivot point around which turn all the elaborate philosophies and practices that together make up the spiritual life of India.

From the Buddhist point of view, the salient feature of a dream is that it is not real in the way it appears. The dream is real in a sense—it is a real dream—but its true nature is veiled as it masquerades as waking life. When I'm dreaming, I experience myself as an individual moving through a world populated with objects and people separate from me. But the truth is that there is no real difference between the "I" and the objects or other people—it's all an effect of the imagination, a vivid fantasy. To be lost in a dream means, then, to be unaware that the perceived distinction between "me" and "not me" is an illusion created by the mind.

So it is that when I wake up in the morning, I say to myself *It was all just a dream*, and I marvel at how profoundly I was deceived while I slept. Then I get out of bed and go about my business, with no suspicions whatsoever about the nature of my waking experience. True, if the dream was especially pleasant or disturbing, then a particular image may lodge itself in my memory so that the feeling of the dream experience lingers, suspended like a faint mist over and around the practical affairs of the day. But the fact that only hours before I was wholly betrayed by my mind—taking imagination for reality—does not, as a rule, provoke me to question the contours of my waking life and its fundamental distinction between self and other.

This is somewhat curious. Where do I derive this unreflective confidence that I and my world are exactly what they seem to be when I am routinely misled in my dreams? What would it require to shake my certainty that things are not as they appear?

Consider, from this perspective, the peculiar experience that psychologists refer to as a "false awakening":

> They can take a number of distinct forms, but in all of these a person believes that he has woken up when he has not. Thus the dreamer may appear to awake realistically in his own bedroom and finds his room, which may seem to be familiar in all its details, around him; and if he does not realize that he is dreaming, a more or less plausible representation of the process of dressing, breakfasting and setting off to work may then follow . . . the environment often appears to be meticulously realistic and the dreamer in a fairly rational state of mind.[76]

Some years ago I talked with a woman who had experienced three false awakenings in a row, one after another. In the first, her alarm sounded, she reached over and turned it off, lay still for a moment, realized she was dreaming, then slipped back into dreamless sleep. In the second, she turned off the alarm, got out of bed, put on her slippers, and was half way down the hall when all over again, she realized she was dreaming then drifted back into deep sleep. The third time she got all the way to the bathroom and was brushing her teeth when she chanced to look up and saw no reflection in the mirror. Just the vacant, polished glass where her face should be. Immediately she awoke, startled, and this time found herself lying in bed. She told me she lay there for quite a while after that, recalling the previous dream episodes, examining her hands, scanning the room for clues. At last, she got up and started her day. And there she was, only a few hours later, telling me all of this.

"How do you know . . . ?" I began, hesitantly, then changed course. "I mean, how *did* you know, the last time it happened, that you were really awake?"

She shrugged her shoulders and grinned sheepishly. "I couldn't just lie there forever."

The border between waking and dream is notoriously porous, as is the border between memory and imagination. It would be more accurate to speak of an "interface" than a "border." But to speak in this way immediately suggests a number of troubling reflections about the nature of reality as conventionally defined through reference to the waking state.

The first thing to notice in this regard is that the difference between waking and dreaming is not a simple matter of reality versus unreality: a dream is not in every respect unreal. As the psychologist and philosopher William James pointed out over a century ago in *The Varieties of Religious Experience*, a dream may be misleading, but it is, after all, undeniably real as a type of first-person experience, similar in this respect to the experience of seeing a hallucination or a mirage. Like the image of water shimmering over hot asphalt, the content of the dream is not real in the way it appears to be, but the raw experience of dreaming is itself uncontestable. Nor, for that matter, is the dreamer necessarily fooled. Just as I can see the pool of water on the road ahead and know it for the mirage that it is, it is also possible to dream and simultaneously to *know* that I am dreaming. The woman I mentioned just above, for example, realized that she was dreaming at some point in each of her false awakening experiences. So-called lucid dreams are, in fact, relatively common. Here's another example, drawn from my own experience.

I once found myself caught up in a weird sensation that things were not as they appeared to be. The setting at the time was picturesque but not especially provocative. I was standing at one end of a spacious room lined with windows opening onto a mountain valley that extended for miles into the distance. Above the peaks the sky was an endless expanse of blue streaked with wisps of cloud. I was looking out the windows when it occurred to me that I might be dreaming. Nothing in particular was unusual about the situation, yet something was not quite right.

How could I confirm my suspicion? I had read about lucid dreams but had never experienced one. And then I recalled that in one of the books I had read, the author suggested that if I think that I might be dreaming I can test the hypothesis by attempting to do something I wouldn't be able to do in waking life. Preferably something safe, like levitation. So I turned my attention to a vase that was sitting on a nearby table. Summoning the invisible force of my will, I commanded the vase to move.

To my great astonishment, it wobbled slightly, tilted, then rose an inch or two into the air and glided sideways down along the surface of the table, picking up speed and altitude as it went, held loosely in the grip of my conscious gaze. Lofting it into the air was one thing; managing its trajectory was, as I soon discovered, quite another. It was a bit like trying to steer a floater—one of those gray specks that migrate listlessly through the open space in front of your eyes. When I looked directly at the vase it would dart away. In order to control its movement I had to keep it in my peripheral vision, being careful not to move my eyes too quickly. Honing this method, I was able to gently swing the arc of my visual field, dragging the vase behind so that it passed through the air and across the room, full circle, settling once again where it had been before, there on the table.

I was thrilled. As the realization that I was dreaming sunk in and it became increasingly apparent that things were not real in the way they appeared to be real, they paradoxically became even more real than they had ever been before, but in a way I could never have imagined. In the aura of my excitement, the whole world lit up. Colors became extraordinarily intense, shapes and textures blossomed around me like exotic flowers. It felt as if everything were newly created, emerging from the void literally as I watched. Or had it always been that way, and I only now noticed? It was then that I saw I was not alone. Over in one corner three men stood facing each other in a tight circle, engaged in muted conversation. Immediately I went over to them and interrupted their discussion.

"This is a *dream*," I blurted out, unable to restrain my enthusiasm. "I'm dreaming! This is a dream!"

They quit talking, turned in my direction, and regarded me with baleful consternation, clearly not pleased at the intrusion.

"All of you . . ." I stammered, suddenly cognizant of their reaction, "all of *us* . . . we're in a dream! It's amazing!"

They looked at me as if I were mad.

"You don't believe me." I said. "But it's true. Watch this." I glanced sideways at the vase, now some distance away, and made it rise and float. The men stood placidly observing. One of them rolled his eyes, ever so slightly. After a few seconds they turned away and resumed their conversation.

That's the last thing I recall from my dream.

Remarkable as it was, in most respects my lucid dream experience was not at all unique. To know that one is dreaming—to be awake in the dream—alters, in an essential way, the nature of the experience. In a full-blown lucid dream, such as the one I had, the dream world, oddly enough, often feels *more* real than normal waking life, and this sense of heightened reality provokes a feeling of awe or wonder at the mere fact of existence, the utter strangeness of the ordinary. And of course one can do things—like levitate a vase—that would be impossible in waking life because they would violate the so-called laws of nature. Nevertheless, even in a lucid dream one does not have complete control; there is always an element of the experience that lies beyond the range of the dreamer's will. In my case, for instance, I could not compel those three men to share in my astonishment. Displaying the magic of the dream world was not sufficient to warrant their interest. Of course they were dream people, at home in that world, so perhaps they had witnessed such things countless times before and had long since started taking them for granted, as we take for granted the imponderable mystery of the world we inhabit.

How does all this bear on the question I posed above, the central question of Buddhism? What does it mean to say that Prince Gautama *woke up*?

Just as a false awakening leaves one lost in the dream without knowing it—still fooled, that is, by the apparent division between self and other—so, according to the Buddha's teaching, we experience a similar kind of false awakening every morning. Like the woman who only imagined she was awake, we transition from one dream to another, chagrined at how we were taken in by the first without suspecting that we are now wandering lost in a second—namely, in this dream of birth and death, where an isolated, independent self appears to struggle for control in a world of fixed, immutable objects. The essence of a false awakening is to imagine you have left the dream behind when in fact you have not. The Buddha, however, awakened not *from* the dream of life but rather *in* it; his awakening is analogous in this respect to the experience of a lucid dream. To falsely awaken *from* a dream is to move from one misconception to another; to wake up *in* a dream, however, is to see the illusion for what it is without any sense of leaving it behind.

Still, the analogy only goes so far. And where the analogy loses traction is precisely where things take on a characteristically Buddhist flavor no longer fully amenable to rational explanation.

Here is the difficulty: Everything about a lucid dream is experienced as illusory, but there is nevertheless an outside world where I am asleep in bed. Moreover, in the dream I know as much, and this knowledge provides a fixed reference point: the dream is illusory or unreal only *in comparison* with the reality of waking experience. The "I" within the dream may be mere fantasy, but that fantasy consciously refers back to the "I" of the dreamer—the person who will eventually wake up and get out of bed and carry on. For a buddha, however—one who has awakened within the waking dream of birth and death—there is no touchstone to another world, no other reality in comparison with which *this* is an illusion, and no other self apart from the self in the dream. For a buddha there is only our present experience, and our present experience is a dream that refers back to nowhere and no one, to nothing and nobody.

To "wake up" in this peculiar sense means to see present experience as a ship without an anchor, an "experience" that is not really an experience at all, for it has no subjective or objective ground. This, I suggest, is the import of this notoriously enigmatic line from the *Descent into Lanka Sutra*: "Things are not as they appear, nor are they otherwise."[77] The story of the Buddha's awakening implies the possibility of a gestalt shift in our attitude toward the ordinary day-to-day world, which he perceived to be in some profound sense both inherently deceptive and, at the same time, entirely sufficient unto itself and worthy of unsparing love.

What the Buddha discovered must remain, from our present perspective, an unimaginable marvel hidden, as the saying goes, right here before our eyes, here where crimson and yellow-gold leaves drift past my window, twirling in the pristine light of a late October afternoon, here in this world of fierce beauty and sorrow, where we delight in our gifts, and suffer, and die.

"We see and see," says the Gospel of Mark, "but do not perceive; we hear and hear, but do not understand."[78]

And yet . . . we can wonder.

The woman who dreamed three times in succession that she had woken up was right: we can't just lie in bed waiting to figure out once and for all what's real and what's not. As if such a feat were even possible. The problem is, this whole elaborate business of the self and its world hangs—or falls—together, so we can never know with any certainty who or even where we are. We can only know what *seems* to be true. But what difference does it make, really, whether we ourselves and the people and things we experience actually exist in some objective fashion or only appear to do so? One way or another, we have to get up and pack the kids off to school, clean the house, go to work, pay the bills.

And yet we yearn to know more than what merely seems, to find something in this fleeting world that we can safely call our own, something, or someone, to have and hold. We yearn to experience more or other than what we've been given. The Buddha's awakening, as I've characterized it here, offers no promise of fulfilling that particular dream. I think of the Japanese poet Kobayashi Issa, who wrote, on the death of his newborn child:

Tsuyu no yo wa
tsuyu no yo nagara
sarinagara

This world of dew
is only the world of dew—
and yet . . . oh and yet . . .[79]

A Pathless Land

Nothing happens? Or has everything happened,
and are we standing now, quietly, in the new life?[80]

IF YOU HAVE EVER TRIED to make yourself fall asleep, you'll know what I'm talking about.

Let's imagine it's midnight and you have some kind of high-stakes event early the next morning—a job interview or a big exam. You're stressed and worried, but under the circumstances that's to be expected. You've studied up, gone over all the necessary material, and now what you need more than anything is a good night's sleep so you'll be at your best in the morning. What do you do?

If you're like me, the first thing you do is take care of whatever needs to be taken care of in your home. Depending on your circumstances, that could mean getting the kids in bed, letting the dog out to pee—that sort of thing. Do what needs to be done. When everyone else is settled in and the house is quiet, you might get things ready for the morning. Select the clothes you'll wear, set up the coffee maker. Then you change into your pajamas and maybe sit quietly with a soothing drink—chamomile tea or a cup of hot chocolate. Finally you brush your teeth, go to your bedroom—a place set apart from areas of the house dominated by the energy of daytime activities. There you climb into bed, pull up the covers, make sure the alarm is set, turn out the light, and lie quietly with your eyes closed, waiting to fall asleep.

Most of us follow some version of this routine, adapted to the particulars of our situation. When we want to go to sleep, we probably choose to replace, as much as possible, bright light and noise with darkness and silence, or perhaps with comforting images and sounds. For infants or toddlers, there are white noise machines. For some adults, the flickering images and superficial banter of late-night television can accomplish a similar purpose, especially when the volume is low. Nowadays there are even podcasts designed explicitly for the purpose of coaxing people toward sleep. The narrator's voice drones on in a monotone, more or less incoherently, gliding in and out of a story line that seems like it might be headed somewhere but never quite arrives.

One thing, however, is certain: getting to sleep can't be achieved simply through the exercise of willpower. I can't make myself go to sleep. I can only, so to speak, take myself to the very edge of waking, and once there, let go. That's why we call it *falling* asleep.

And therein lies the problem: the path to the edge is relatively clear, but how exactly do I make myself let go?

There are other, similar "falling type" experiences that are ultimately outside my control. For example, let's say I'm going to see a comedian perform. I hail a cab, go to the club, and pay the cover, but once there I cannot *make* myself laugh. If the comic isn't funny, or I'm in a foul mood, I'll just sit there feeling angry or disappointed. If I'm with other people and feeling social pressure, I can of course pretend to laugh, but fake laughter is no more satisfying than fake sleep. Pretending to laugh or sleep is no substitute for the real thing. What I crave is not a facsimile but the genuine article: a solid night's rest, the kind of laughter that has me braying and snorting, tears streaming from my eyes. That alone is truly worth the price of admission.

In a similar fashion, I can open myself to the possibility of falling in love, but there's no way I can make it happen. To be clear, I'm not just talking about romantic love. Before the birth of my son—that is to say, from the vantage point of a forty-five-year-old ruthlessly independent, self-centered white male who had lived more or less on his own terms ever since leaving his parents' home—when I contemplated becoming a parent, all I could envision was a crushing responsibility that would curtail my personal freedom in myriad unacceptable ways. But I knew that my wife wanted children; it was part of the deal when we got married. So, with considerable apprehension, I opened myself to the eventuality of becoming a parent. I had no idea how being a father would utterly transform my priorities (how it continues to utterly transform my priorities). I anticipated the loss of personal freedom, but I could never have imagined beforehand what it would mean to love a child, what a relief it would be to see the center of gravity in my life shift so dramatically from a preoccupation with my own self-centered needs and desires to an unreflective concern with the needs and desires of this other, small person (and, soon enough, his sister). In other words, I *fell* in love, and when it happened, it was both spontaneous and effortless.

Sleep. Laughter. Love.

There is something profoundly satisfying—even essential—about such experiences, and yet they are ultimately outside our control. No matter how much I want or even need to fall into sleep or laughter or love, I can't force it to happen through the power of will because sleep, laughter, and love are, in essence, moments of surrender not subject to coercion. They are, in some fundamental sense, *given*. That is, moments of surrender either simply happen, unforced, or they don't. There is some elusive higher power at work here, some enigmatic, elemental force that hints at the Christian notion of grace. To fall asleep, to laugh at a good joke, or to be swept away by affection for another person is to be granted an utterly spontaneous blessing. And yet, paradoxically, at the very moment this blessing is conferred, there is no one present to receive it, since what is surrendered in that moment is my very self. In that instant of self-surrender, the sense of agency that lies at the core of my habitual, deep-seated experience of myself as an independent, isolated individual gives way and tumbles over the edge of the precipice, melting into the vast, empty space of an ultimately groundless universe.

To return to a point made in a previous chapter, even though I have referred to falling asleep, falling into laughter, and falling in love as experiences, they are not really "experiences" in the customary meaning of the word, which implies a distinction between the subject—the one who experiences—and an object—what is experienced. Simply put, where there is no self, there is no possibility of experience. This peculiar "falling" is, then, best understood not as a kind of novel experience but rather as an emancipation from experience, a freedom from the known.

As we grow, the ego or personality coalesces around a sense of agency. To be *somebody* is to have the capacity to make things happen, to take control of a situation and shape it to the dictates of my will. Politicians and entrepreneurs—experts at making things happen—are regarded as powerful, important people who are successful in life. We often admire such people because they accomplish big things and are rewarded for it with fame, status, and money. And yet this same conviction—that I am in essence an actor who can and must *make* things happen by exerting my will—becomes a prison. Ironically, the only desire as persistent and fundamental as the desire to act out of self-interest in order to achieve some goal and reap the benefits is its exact opposite: the desire to be free of the burden of the self and its endless fretting over status or money or power. But the more I long to be free of myself, the more such freedom eludes my grasp, because that very longing comes to define and therefore strengthen the ego.

Of course Buddhism is about waking up—not falling asleep—but it might be more accurate in this case to speak of *falling awake*, since Buddhist awakening is the paradigm of total, unreserved, and artless self-surrender. The desire to fall awake is a peculiar form of desire: a desire to cease desiring. And the path to awakening—to the extent that there is one—must embody a similarly contradictory form of striving: the striving to not strive. There is simply no way I can win at this game. The harder I twist and pull, the tighter the knot gets. At some point my only choice is to give up trying to not try, which is, of course, no choice at all. Giving up, as it turns out, is one thing I simply cannot choose to do. It is entirely outside the scope of my will.

Among Buddhist philosophers an ancient controversy revolves around the question of whether awakening comes about gradually, over time, or all at once, in a sudden flash of insight. There were those who suggested that both are true. Just as a peach begins as a hard, bitter fruit fastened tightly to the branch from which it hangs, so one's sense of self takes shape in childhood and, if all goes well, matures as the years pass, growing firm and confident, holding tightly to the patterns of behavior and belief that nurture its inherent authority. But when one commits to a long-term monogamous relationship, or to parenting, or to spiritual practice, like the peach slowly ripening in the warm sun, this same sense of self gradually softens. Bit by bit the mind relaxes its grip on everything that formally provided it with the illusion of security until, finally, one day it simply lets go of the branch and falls.

If we look closely enough, with a patient eye for the subtle forces that are constantly at work in this ripening process, we would presumably see the fibers in the stem stretching and giving way, one by one, steadily moving toward the point when that last, single thread snaps and the ripe peach falls from the tree. Nevertheless, however long it might take to arrive, there's nothing gradual about the moment when that last, microscopic fiber gives way. The instant when the mind finally lets loose of its compulsive need to feel in control—to make things happen or not happen—is both unpredictable and essentially timeless. Ripening is one thing; falling is another. If the fruit drops at all, it drops *now*. And this is precisely where the allegory fails, as must all our efforts to rationalize the spiritual life, for there simply is no self other than the one that clings to the branch. Absent clinging, there is no fruit to fall, no self to *let go*. But we cling. We lie awake all night worrying. We resent the demands our spouse or children make on our time and energy. The days and weeks go by, summer turns to fall, fall to winter. A whole lifetime passes. Snow falls and the fruit just hangs there, a withered, black knob clinging to the bare branch.

The Indian mystic Krishnamurti once famously declared, in a speech delivered to hundreds of members of the Theosophical Society who regarded him as an incarnation of God, that truth is a pathless land. And indeed, just as some problems will not yield to rational analysis, so there are skills that cannot be learned by mastering a formula. What sort of rote training could allow us to give ourselves over without reservation to this evidently less than perfect world, a world where—to grossly understate the matter—events so often simply do not conform to our deepest wishes. The everyday frustrations of family life, friends, and work are a constant and unremitting threat to the ego's striving for happiness and fulfillment. And in the face of what the philosopher Mark Johnston calls the large-scale structural defects of human life—"arbitrary suffering, the decay of corrosive aging, our profound ignorance of our condition, the isolation produced by ordinary self-involvement, the vulnerability of everything we cherish to time and chance, and, finally, to untimely death"[81]—is it even possible to imagine a life worth living without some degree of self-deception? It seems to me that any prescribed response to this question must be either trivial or presumptuous. If there is—for lack of a better word—some kind of genuine reconciliation to be found, anything like redemption, then it must emerge from a deeply personal struggle, a struggle that is fundamentally different for each of us. So how are we to interpret the Buddhist claim to present a "path to awakening"? Can I really learn how to make myself fall awake by following a set of fixed rules applicable to anyone?[82]

I referred above to the ancient Buddhist controversy about whether awakening is achieved gradually or all at once. There is as well a third alternative: awakening isn't *achieved* at all. The Mahayana tradition has always maintained, in one way or another, that there is nothing to accomplish. The idea is baldly asserted in the *Heart Sutra*;[83] it is also strongly implied in Nagarjuna's baffling declaration that there is not the slightest difference between samsara and nirvana, suffering and its end, delusion and wisdom.[84] But perhaps the most transparent illustration of this teaching is found in a Mahayana doctrine according to which all sentient beings possess buddha nature (identified in Dzogchen with "naturally occurring timeless awareness"). In the Tibetan Dzogchen and Chinese and Japanese Chan/Zen traditions, the implications of this doctrine are spelled out in a parade of confounding practices designed to make it clear, in the most dramatic terms, that there is nothing whatsoever to strive for, since underneath or behind all the striving we are already—just as we are—fully awakened buddhas.

One way of interpreting this might be to suggest that our awakened nature is implicitly present in our very striving. It is present in the restless dissatisfaction that judges and rejects as unsuitable the fleeting things of this world. In this sense, our dis-ease may be said to find its source in the fissure between who I mistakenly think I am and who, in fact, I am *not*, between "conscious empirical self-hood and the preexisting depths of one's being."[85] For it is from these preexisting depths that the intuition of inviolable truth and beauty emerges and becomes fixed in discursive thought as an ideal to be attained through some kind of exotic "spiritual experience." In which case the fissure exists only in my fevered imagination, where I am constantly struggling to find what is already present, to experience what is, in essence, altogether beyond experience, or—one might say—what is implicit in every experience, even the most ordinary and mundane.

At any rate, for the astute Zen or Dzogchen disciple, the secret is out: there is nothing to accomplish, no final reward to be claimed. That we are incapable of seeing this is precisely the problem. In our obsessive quest to experience something strange and glamorous—to become someone other than who we are, to have something we don't presently have—we manufacture the causes of our own suffering. In the Mahayana, the striving to fall awake is a deeply ironic endeavor, and all this business about a path leading to a final goal is nothing more than "skillful means"—an indispensable trick or charade designed to appeal, initially, to my most deluded, selfish instincts and to focus those instincts on the desire to save myself by attaining a spiritual goal—namely, nirvana or awakening. As one's practice deepens and one's understanding of Buddhist doctrine becomes more nuanced, this conception of the path is increasingly seen to be riddled with contradiction; the idea of awakening as an exotic experience to be attained or achieved is gradually revealed as a kind of mirage, something that only *seems* to be true from the perspective of a self that only *seems* to exist. As David Higgins explains, summarizing the Dzogchen perspective:

> Although the individual must initially rely on stages of learning (*lam rim*) and aspire intellectually and ethically

> toward invariant modes of being and awareness (*sku dang ye shes*), this abiding mode increasingly takes over as mind's obscuring superimpositions, including the heuristic fictions of paths and levels, fall away. It is precisely at this point where the elaborate architecture of mind falls apart that primordial awareness reveals itself. In soteriological terms, this breaking point marks the transition from the progressive paths of mind to the non-traversable path of primordial knowing, a path that is simply the living present, having no pre-established starting point, route or destination.[86]

There's a catch here, though, and it's a very big one: this only *seeming* to be true—seeming, that is, *as if* there were a real, individual self with something to achieve—is in some way we can never quite grasp, inescapable. Put it however you like: There is no solid ground under our feet, no fixed reality underlying the mirage. The mirage of the self and its world is all there is. The only reality is the reality of appearances. Once again, this is the gist of that enigmatic line from the *Descent into Lanka Sutra* that I cited above: "Things are not as they seem, nor are they otherwise." In this sense the idea of a path leading to a goal is an illusion, but it's a necessary illusion, an illusion that fools us in ways we need to be fooled but can neither anticipate, nor escape, or fully comprehend. The relationship between what only seems to be and the deeper truth that in some mysterious fashion what only seems to be is all we have, is similar to the relationship between Newtonian physics—where the sensual, physical world is all there is—and quantum physics, which reveals the ever-deeper truths that this physical world only seems to be real in the way we imagine it to be and that behind the appearance of the physical is something more true or real—the atoms and protons and "strings," the winding coils of DNA, the synapses firing in the brain, and all those hormones that shape our emotional life.

All of this is unavailable to our senses; these are truths accessible only through our ever more sophisticated technologies and the scientific theories based on what they reveal. David Abram expresses the perplexing relationship between these two truths—the sensual and the scientific—in a particularly vivid way:

> Every coherent image we can have of those other, ostensibly more objective dimensions of reality is secretly rooted . . . in the ambiguous, ever-shifting terrain of our ordinary experience. Everything we have come to believe about those presumably more fundamental scales of reality is tacitly dependent upon our everyday engagement with the world at *this* scale—the very scale of existence to which our animal senses are tuned. In the open expanse of our full-bodied experience, the entities that meet our senses are not quarks and protons, but rather brambles and mushroom and slowly eroding hillsides; not DNA base pairs or neuronal synapse but rather children, and woodpeckers, and the distant sound of thunder. Although we regularly try to explain the ambiguous world by appealing to those more mathematically precise realms hidden behind the perceivable surroundings, it is ultimately our ongoing relation to the capricious earth that holds the key to all those abstract and provisional worlds.[87]

In focusing his attention on the realm of the sensual and visible, Abram tends to downplay the equally valid truth that just as the intangible realm of subatomic physics is concealed within and dependent upon the physical world in which we live and breathe, so the physical is inextricably embedded within and entirely dependent upon the intangible realm of subatomic physics. The unseen is hidden within the seen, just as the seen is hidden within the unseen. In a similar fashion, nothingness is concealed in everything, and everything is concealed in nothing.

Neither the seen nor the unseen is any more or less real than the other, though they appear to physicists as irreconcilably different realities. Einstein died searching for a unified field theory that would bring these two worlds together under a single mathematical theory. Buddhism, however, is based on the premise that the invisible "nothingness" at the core of everything is not a strictly conceptual, abstract, or theoretical realm. Rather this nothingness can be directly experienced in a way analogous to our immediate experience of the physical, sensual world.

If you're having trouble figuring this out, that's because you can't. The relationship between what Buddhism refers to as ultimate and conventional truth is considered to be one of the most abstruse subjects in Buddhist philosophy precisely because it is not amenable to any purely rational explanation. We simply must act *as if* physical objects really exist as they appear to exist, all the while knowing they do not. Similarly, we must act as if there really is a path and a goal, even though there isn't. You must follow the path that is not a path so you can see for yourself that it leads nowhere or, perhaps more precisely, that it leads back to exactly where you started. You must wake up *in* the dream in order to see the dream for what it is, to see that waking up is itself, in some inexplicable manner, an illusion, because there never was anything other than the dream.

This extraordinarily elusive quality of "seeming as if" is manifest in a particularly abstruse fashion in the finely grained language of Nagarjuna's brilliant masterwork, the *Fundamental Verses on the Middle Way*, the single most influential composition in the entire Mahayana corpus and the epitome of what I just referred to as necessary illusion or skillful means. Over the centuries logicians of various stamps—most recently, analytic philosophers—have been drawn to this text, both captivated and vexed by what appear to be coherent arguments leading to some kind of conclusion but are in fact snares for the rational, grasping mind, bottomless conundrums that frustrate its every attempt to find some kind of conceptual ground on which to take a stand. It is a work of indisputable genius that resists any simple categorization as either "religious" or "philosophical" writing. In fact the text does not comfortably fit into any recognized Western genre. Nagarjuna's opus is certainly not a logical treatise in the modern analytic sense—a series of arguments intended solely to establish conceptual clarity and literal, propositional truth. This is so notwithstanding the claims made by the exponents of a form of logic called dialetheism, who maintain in their interpretation of Nagarjuna that propositional truth—when properly exploited so as to accommodate "real contradictions"—can take us to the limits of language and thought and beyond. All of this eminently reasonable discourse is simply piling one assertion on top of another in an unending attempt to have the final word, to fashion the correct, winning argument. But it will never happen. No logician will ever have the final word on Nagarjuna for the simple reason that, as Nagarjuna himself clearly saw, it's impossible to reason your way out of reason. Chandrakirti, Nagarjuna's most famous classical commentator, cites a verse that speaks directly to this point:

> The Buddha taught that nirvana is itself no-nirvana;
> a knot tied by space can only be untied by space.[88]

Nagarjuna has offered us a knot tied by space, and it will never be untied by reason alone. In its futile efforts to untie Nagarjuna's knot that is no-knot, rational argumentation merely throws into relief its own self-imposed limitations, which is exactly what Nagarjuna's "arguments" are designed to do. No doubt rational argumentation has played an integral role in the history of Buddhist thought by exploring a range of epistemological and ontological problems related to basic doctrinal teachings, but as applied to the interpretation of Nagarjuna, it takes on the aspect of a powerful engine thrown out of gear, all that energy uncoupled from any concrete purpose and set adrift. For a dialetheist, we are told, "concepts proliferate everywhere"—even *beyond* the so-called "limits of language and thought."[89]

The lesson I take from this is quite simple: from a strictly logical point of view, there really are no limits to language and thought other than those one can talk and think about. But from a soteriological point of view, the limits of language and thought are very real; such limits are reached and surpassed only when all the arguing and reasoning—with its abject reliance on literal, referential language—is finally seen to be a hindrance to going deeper, and so is put away. I'm reminded of Alan Watts's quip about hallucinogens: "When you get the message, hang up the phone." The logicians for whom concepts proliferate everywhere evidently have not yet gotten the message. Or maybe they have (who am I to say?), and yet, like good Anglo-American analytic philosopher-bodhisattvas, they nevertheless keep thinking and talking and arguing with one another to help out those who can benefit from their labored attempts to determine whose view is right and whose view is wrong. We benefit by seeing for ourselves how all this logical discourse is valuable precisely *because* it ultimately fails to connect with Nagarjuna's soteriological purpose.

In any case, it seems to me much better simply to begin with the understanding that Nagarjuna has nothing to prove, no propositional truth to assert or defend (which he himself explicitly states), and go on to read the *Fundamental Verses on the Middle Way* as a manual for contemplative practice, a highly sophisticated inducement to leave behind attachment to the vagaries of discursive thought in all its manifestations—including reasoned argument—and so to clear the way for a profound silence accessed at the vanishing point of mind, in the "preexisting depths of one's being." When read from this perspective, not as a species of philosophical argumentation leading to a firm conclusion but rather as the *disclosure* or *exhibition*—the *acting out*—of a radical surrender of the very desire to know, Nagarjuna's masterwork becomes a dazzling rhetorical performance, full of sound and fury, signifying nothing.[90]

We have reached a place where words can no longer be counted on to have concrete meaning, even when they seem as if they must. In this shadowy terrain, literal, referential language no longer suffices as a guide. We are compelled to rely on metaphor, innuendo, and allusion as the most effective means to elicit the intuition of a truth that is no truth, an unreal reality, a dream *from* which we cannot awaken. To wake up not from but *in* the dream of life and death is to see both that nothing is real in the way it appears and, at the same time, that appearance is all we have. After all—lest we forget—the idea of "awakening" is itself a trope, and the Buddha—the Awakened One—nothing more or less than the idealized embodiment of a metaphor. In fact, the language of Mahayana Buddhism is entirely reliant on metaphor, either implicitly, as with Nagarjuna's "arguments," or explicitly, as, for instance, in this poem by the Japanese Zen poet Taigu Ryokan:

Too lazy to be ambitious,
I let the world take care of itself.
Ten days' worth of rice in my bag;
a bundle of twigs by the fireplace.
Why chatter about delusion and enlightenment?
Listening to the night rain on my roof,
I stretch out my legs and relax.[91]

Ryokan is having a bit of fun with us, for he obviously knows that without the chatter about delusion and enlightenment there would be no poem. He's playing a very sophisticated game, writing poetry that seems to want to use language to transcend language, to say what cannot be said. Once we see what he's up to, we begin to sense the subtle ambiguity of his poem that simultaneously affirms and denies the value of chattering in a way that eludes any rational accounting. Similarly, like the man lying fast asleep in bed dreaming he is awake, fretting and worrying in his dream about how he can't sleep, we chatter on about delusion and enlightenment, samsara and nirvana, path and goal, moving through our days craving a more perfect, more "spiritual" life. If only we could wake up, not from the dream but *in* it—right here in this sad and beautiful world of endless, unfathomable wonder—we would see that we already have everything we need. And what we need seems—in some inscrutable way—to include a whole lot of chattering: the chattering of the Buddha, of Nagarjuna and Ryokan, of poetry and literature, philosophy and religion, and even the chattering of the logicians, as well as the chattering of a book like this one, which seems to want to explain a mystery that can't be explained but can only be shown, and *is* shown, by only seeming to explain.[92]

Coming Home

What we choose to fight is so tiny!
What fights with us is so great!
If only we would let ourselves be dominated
as things do by some immense storm,
we would become strong too, and not need names.[93]

WHAT ACT OF HUBRIS could possibly exceed the attempt to write about nirvana? If the dearth of comments in early Buddhist scripture can be taken as a reliable guide, then even the Buddha himself was reluctant to speak on the subject. And yet there it is, the third noble truth, enshrined at the very center of his teaching in the simplest possible terms: nirvana is the end of dis-ease (*duhkha*). And bringing dis-ease to an end is the goal of all Buddhist practice. What's implied here? It's a question we can't avoid.

To appreciate what is meant by *dis-ease* in this context, one must imagine, however vaguely, what might pass for its absence. According to the second noble truth, our chronic dis-ease is rooted in an insatiable thirst (*trishna*) for something more or better than what our present experience offers. We are simply unable, or unwilling, to accept life on its own terms, which leaves us forever unsatisfied and anxious. Nirvana, conceived as the remedy for this dis-ease through the eradication of its cause, would then appear to be not so much an end to all my problems but rather a kind of fundamental contentment or peace amid those problems, a profound reconciliation with the world as it is. Something along the lines of what is expressed in the famous "serenity prayer" attributed to Reinhold Niebuhr:

> God, give me grace to accept with serenity
> the things that cannot be changed,
> courage to change the things
> that should be changed,
> and the wisdom to distinguish
> the one from the other.
>
> Living one day at a time,
> enjoying one moment at a time,
> accepting hardship as a pathway to peace,
> taking, as Jesus did,
> this sinful world as it is,
> not as I would have it,
> trusting that you will make all things right
> if I surrender to your will,
> so that I may be reasonably happy in this life
> and supremely happy with you forever in the next.
> Amen.

A moving and powerful prayer. Buddhism is not, however, a theological religion, nor is nirvana formulated as a "supreme happiness" confined to an afterlife in some other, heavenly world. Nirvana is a serenity presumed to be attainable here, in the midst of our immediate, day-to-day tribulations—amid, that is, "things that cannot be changed." Or so it would seem, since that is apparently what Prince Gautama discovered when he became the Buddha. According to the canonical story, he remained on earth for forty-five years after his awakening, teaching and leading the Buddhist monastic community.

In any case, absent the possibility of God's grace, it's not hard to see that there is a problem with this picture: to desire serenity or contentment is to desire to stop desiring what you don't have, it is to thirst for an end to thirst, which is futile. The desire to stop desiring is evidently just another form of desire; so as long as one desires to stop desiring, one will never cease desiring. How can desire put an end to itself? But then, how is one ever going to stop desiring without first desiring to stop? And isn't the whole point of the Buddha's teaching to meticulously define the problem of desire, and in doing so to make us *want* to bring our habitual dis-satisfaction to an end?

This conundrum lies at the heart of Buddhist doctrine and practice. Nevertheless, Buddhism would not be Buddhism without the promise of nirvana as the end of dis-ease and thirst. Moreover, in the *Udana*—a section of the Pali canon that includes some of the oldest extant Buddhist scriptures—we find several places where the Buddha characterizes nirvana in positive terms, as something other than a mere absence. Here is one:

> There is, monks, an unborn, unbecome, uncreated, unconditioned. If there were no unborn, unbecome, unmade, unconditioned there would be no possibility of freedom from what is born, become, created, conditioned. Because there is, monks, an unborn, unbecome, uncreated, unconditioned, there is the possibility of freedom from what is born, become, created, conditioned.[94]

Our world is marked by birth and death, by constant change, an unending cycle of success and failure, gain and loss. My presence here as an individual, and the presence of every other living being, is fleeting and tenuous, conditioned as it is by an infinitely complex and fragile web of interrelationships that determine the biological, sociological, and psychological aspects of personhood. The same is of course true for insentient objects: they arise and pass away in dependence on an endless flux of circumstantial factors. Barring supernatural intervention, it's difficult to see how this world could offer any real, lasting peace. Yet this description of nirvana seems to suggest that there is, right here with us and yet unseen, a separate, more desirable world, or perhaps the portal to such a world. As if this world held within itself the key to a mysterious realm unfazed by the passing of time and the presence of circumstances and things beyond our control. As if our present existence were both what it appears to be and, at the same time, something else entirely.

In another passage from the same scripture, the Buddha tells a gathering of monks,

> When there is dependence on another, there is anxiety; when there is no dependence on another, there is no anxiety. When there is no anxiety, there is tranquility; when there is tranquility, there is no taking sides. When there is no taking sides, there is no coming and going. When there is no coming and going, there is no death and rebirth. When there is no death and rebirth, there is no here or there or any place between. Just this is the end of dis-ease.[95]

This chain of associations links access to the enigmatic, unconditioned realm of nirvana with the cultivation of equanimity and calmness, affective states that presumably emerge when one becomes detached from the vicissitudes of one's troubled relationships with others, both sentient and insentient. He seems to be saying—to put it bluntly—that when one withdraws interest from this world of pleasure and pain and seeks a spiritual home elsewhere, one realizes the unconditioned peace of nirvana.

All of this makes me think of a lovely story by Elizabeth Crane called "Football."[96] It begins, "In my next life I want to explain homecoming to someone, enthusiastically."

> I want to understand what it means to say that something is the size of a football field and I want an older brother named Jimmy who plays tight end and I want to know the names of all the players and I want them to carry me over their heads to the bus and I want to eat pizza with them after the game. I

> want to go to all the home games and all the away games and wear blue eyeliner and use Sun-In and I want to make out under the bleachers and I want to wear the halfback's jacket. I want to squint in the bright lights and bring a thick plaid blanket and something hot in a thermos and I want to see my breath as I scream Rah or Whoo or Go team for the Tigers or the Hawks or the Wildcats. I want Jimmy to get a football scholarship to State and I want to call my dad Pop and I want to beg Pop to lend me his pickup to drive downstate to my brother's games . . .

The story continues in this fashion, virtually every sentence beginning with *I want.* We never learn the narrator's name, but we come to know her family and friends, the people who populate the small town where she grew up, a town "where there's nothing to do, where people join bowling leagues and chain-smoke and drink too much and get into fights at bars or get pregnant at the wrong time or by the wrong guy and dream of getting out." But the narrator doesn't get out. More to the point, she doesn't even dream of getting out.

Her life could not be more ordinary. She loses her virginity in a car, graduates from high school, gets a job at the local insurance company, marries her boyfriend, then quits work and raises three children—Jason, Jenny, and Joe—in a house with "a cement patio in back and pink impatiens on the front walk and a basketball hoop over the garage." There is plenty to be happy about here, an ample supply of modest pleasures. But there is as well another, darker side to the story.

Early on the narrator's brother Jimmy gets suspended from the football team for "an 'incident' with a coed," and his life quickly spirals downward.

> When he drives his car into a telephone pole at ninety miles an hour and says it was an accident I want to believe him . . . no matter how sad he looks to be awake the next day. I want to tell Jimmy everything's going to be okay and I want to tell him this for fifteen years while he goes from job to job and

> leaves town and comes back and when Jimmy straightens up so to speak and joins a church and marries a girl from the church who always smiles I want to tell him I'm proud of him even though his eyes look flat now, like Jimmy's skipped class and he's not coming back.

Her husband, Bill, falls for one of his clients ("I want him to come close to having an affair . . . I want to suspect this is going on and then I want to tell myself I'm wrong"). At fourteen, her daughter becomes anorexic ("I want Jenny . . . to eat one lettuce leaf for dinner and I want her to join a program"). One of her two sons is an addict ("I want to send him to rehab twice before he turns seventeen and tell him I'm sorry if I messed him up"). And then, she loses her parents.

> I want Mom to die of old age or a heart attack or anything but cancer and I want Pop to die in his sleep a few months later and I want to tell people he died from a broken heart and I want them to nod when I say it and I want to bury Mom and Pop together by the church and put daisies on their graves once a month and tell them about Jason and Jenny and Joe and I want to know without a doubt they're always with me.

Some years later Bill passes away and, grieving his loss, she drifts into a relationship with her first high school boyfriend. At the end we find her lying in bed, dying. It's then we discover that this whole monologue has been the narrator's retrospective on a life now nearly over. The story closes with a final desire:

> In my next life I want to accept things as they are and when people ask Why I want to say What do you mean why and when everyone comes back for homecoming I want to already be home.

What I find most captivating about Crane's story is the way the protagonist's constant desire is always already fulfilled—so much so that it is ultimately impossible to distinguish what she wants from what she already has, or had, or will have. The life she so desires—*my next life*—is precisely the life she has just lived, is living now, with all its attendant joys and sorrows, down to the last trifling detail. In this anonymous woman's experience, desire and its satisfaction are strangely—one might almost say *miraculously*—inseparable.

In quite another context the philosopher Friedrich Nietzsche articulated a strikingly similar vision. The famous passage I have in mind is found in *The Joyful Wisdom*:

> The greatest weight.—What if some day or night a demon were to steal after you into your loneliest loneliness and say to you: "This life as you now live it and have lived it, you will have to live once more and innumerable times more; and there will be nothing new in it, but every pain and every joy and every thought and sigh and everything unutterably small or great in your life will have to return to you, all in the same succession and sequence—even this spider and this moonlight between the trees, and even this moment and I myself. The eternal hourglass of existence is turned upside down again and again, and you with it, speck of dust!" Would you not throw yourself down and gnash your teeth and curse the demon who spoke thus? . . . Or how well disposed would you have to become to yourself and to life *to crave nothing more fervently* than this ultimate eternal confirmation and seal?[97]

Nietzsche's oracular, strident prose is nothing like the voice of Elizabeth Crane's almost whimsical narrator; what is taken for granted in the unpretentious musing of Crane's nameless housewife is presented by the eminent German atheist as an inconceivably difficult challenge, a brutal exercise of the will. "How well disposed would you have to become to yourself and to life to fervently crave nothing more than what you already have?" Very well disposed indeed. It's unclear whether Nietzsche himself felt such a feat is possible even for his vaunted Übermensch—much less, we can safely assume, for a nondescript American Hausfrau.

But he is clearly aware that merely to appreciate and accept the challenge is in itself transformative.

Here, it seems to me, we may intuit the possibility of a solution to the problem posed by desiring the end of desire. To desire the end of desire is unlike any other form of desire, for it can be understood as a way of actively affirming *what is*. William James, in his classic study *The Varieties of Religious Experience*, conveys as much when he writes,

> The belief is, not that particular events are tempered more towardly to us by a superintending providence, as a reward for our reliance, but that by cultivating the continuous sense of our connection with the power that made things as they are, we are tempered more towardly for their reception. The outward face of nature need not alter, but the expressions of meaning in it alter. It was dead and is alive again. It is like the difference between looking on a person without love, or upon the same person with love. In the latter case intercourse springs into new vitality. So when one's affections keep in touch with the divinity of the world's authorship, fear and egotism fall away; and in the equanimity that follows, one finds in the hours, as they succeed each other, a series of purely benignant opportunities. It is as if all doors were opened, and all paths freshly smoothed.[98]

Again there is the theological language, but James makes it easy to read the phrase "the divinity of the world's authorship" as metaphor, if we so choose. What is important is that in this passage, James makes explicit a set of associations we've encountered throughout this and the preceding chapters. To connect with the power inherent in things as they are—however you conceive of that power, whether it be divine will or Buddhist "suchness"—means to be fully present, here and now: *Living one day at a time, enjoying one moment at a time, accepting hardship as a pathway to peace*. What would otherwise be dead is then alive, transfigured by a love—there is in English no better word for it—that neither denies life's inevitable adversities nor asks for anything more than what is already given. This very world itself then becomes "the realm of the unconditioned," a world no longer laboring under the burden of a personality defined by insatiable, self-centered cravings for a kind of perfection it does not already have. As David Higgins puts it, speaking from the perspective of Tibetan Dzogchen:

> The problem of "finding freedom" . . . is resolved in the recognition that human beings do not *have* freedom but fundamentally *are* free; freedom is not an attribute of a subject, not something we *have*, but the ontological precondition of human existence.[99]

Once more I'm reminded of the serenity prayer with its hope for "a reasonable happiness" in this life and a "supreme happiness" in the next. Perhaps for those who truly accept hardship as a pathway to peace—as many Christian saints and mystics seem to have done, as the Buddha himself did—the gulf between reasonable and supreme happiness is not as wide as it seems. In which case there is no transcendent goal to be attained or achieved, no state of perfection beyond the perfection of what *is*. Through *wanting to not want*—a spiritual practice endorsed not only by Buddhism and Christianity but also by a number of other religions and philosophies—the power of desire might be turned back on itself in a way that makes our altogether earthly experience more than enough. If so, then what we have becomes everything we could wish for.[100]

> How bright and transparent the moonlight of wisdom!
> What is there outside us? What is there we lack?
> Nirvana is openly shown to our eyes.
> This earth where we stand is the pure lotus land!
> And this very body, the body of Buddha.[101]

Letting Go

Before you know what kindness really is
you must lose things,
feel the future dissolve in a moment
like salt in a weakened broth.
What you held in your hand,
what you counted and carefully saved,
all this must go so you know
how desolate the landscape can be
between the regions of kindness.[102]

WHEN I WENT AWAY to India as a young man, I was in search of a wisdom I thought I could not find at home. I had no idea what "wisdom" might be. But now, here at the end of my life, I'm learning.

These days I'm resolutely ensconced at home, an old, dying man living out his last days in quarantine from a pandemic that is ravaging the world. Death, or the threat of death, is everywhere. Here in the silence of my home I'm discovering, as the days pass, that there are distressing truths one can know intellectually but not assimilate, truths one assimilates only when forced down a cul-de-sac. From the perspective of the dead-end road—that prison of necessity—the consequences of not coming to terms with my unmitigated loss (a loss of literally everything) overwhelm my most valiant efforts at denial, all those otiose desires to remain the person I was before being diagnosed with terminal cancer. The truth is, of course, that I will never again be that healthy, vital person; those days are over. I am dying, and what I don't know about death has become a metaphor for what I don't know about life. As I'm compelled to give myself over to this darkness of unknowing, I'm finding a new and deepened understanding about what it means to come to terms with what I've been given—with what Buddhism call the "suchness" (*tathata*) of things.

At the beginning of January 2020—only a few months ago—I was fine. I spent three afternoons every week working out at the gym. I split wood for nightly fires, shoveled the drive, and went for long walks with the dogs, the three of us roaming the woods that blanket thirty acres of land my wife and I own in the hills outside of town. I was eating and drinking and moving through my days with the impunity and self-confidence of a healthy man. I was in fact indulging myself, feasting on a vitality that had followed me into my early seventies. Over the years I had become habituated to my good health, habituated to a body that never failed to respond to my demands. I more or less assumed that tomorrow would be the same as today and that this state of affairs would continue for some time, perhaps another ten years or so. Far enough out, at any rate, that death was nothing more than a vague specter. That, at least, is what insurance actuary tables seemed to promise. The Buddhist texts, with which I was on much more familiar terms, suggested otherwise, but the forces of denial are everywhere reinforced by our popular culture. And we are, after all, creatures of habit, driven by our past karma.

On New Year's Eve my wife and I had invited some guests over to celebrate. We either made or purchased an abundance of wine and liquor and festive treats—rich, heavy fruit cake soaked in rum, a variety of cookies and pastries, a table full of crackers, chips, cheeses, and bowls of creamy dip. In the company of our old and dear friends, we drank, smoked, and talked until sometime after twelve, when one by one people hauled themselves up and out into the cold, snowy darkness, exhausted and ready for bed. It had been a pleasant evening. After they left, my wife and I did some cleaning. When the abandoned plates and glasses and silverware had been rinsed and stacked, ready for washing the next morning, I settled into an armchair to have a nightcap before calling it a day. I had taken the first sip of my bourbon when I noticed stirrings of discomfort rising up from somewhere deep in my gut. Within minutes I was doubled over in excruciating pain. All I could do was press my hands tight against my stomach, curl up on the floor in a fetal position and moan. My wife sat at my side, concerned and vainly trying to comfort me. After half an hour or so the pain began to subside, and I was able to climb the stairs and collapse into bed. This was my first indication that something was not right.

The next morning I woke up with a mild residual discomfort that never went away. The pain was easily bearable, though, and on the fifth of January I went back to teaching. My college has a short, four-week "J-term" that is often used to take students to study abroad. In the past I used to take a group to India every January. It was a lot of work, though, and I eventually got tired of bearing 24/7 responsibility for all the psychological and physical tribulations of ten undergraduate students suddenly plunged into the chaos of South Asia. So I designed a course on the yoga tradition—something I could teach here, on the college's Pine Lake campus, which is what I was doing in January 2020. Every weekday we read and discussed Patanjali's *Yoga Sutras*, practiced hatha yoga, and sat meditation. I felt okay, but the perpetual ache in my stomach remained.

Toward the end of the month, at my wife's prompting, I scheduled an appointment with my family doctor. Worried about possible gallstones, he scheduled me for a sonogram. The procedure was planned for the twenty-eighth of January, a gray Tuesday morning, tiny crystals of snow drifting in frigid air. I had the first appointment of the day. I remember that as I approached the main entrance to the hospital, a crow was perched directly over the doors; as I walked under him he looked down at me, cocked his head to one side, and made a low burbling sound. I was told by a nurse to sit in the waiting room at the hospital while the technicians set up their equipment. I have always disliked the antiseptic, institutional atmosphere of hospitals, and I was anxious to get the test over with so I could return home, where I had work to do to prepare for my spring classes. Only the day before, I had gone to the gym for one of my regular heavy workouts, and I was still basking in the endorphin boost that follows strong physical exertion; a hospital, with sick people being pushed through the linoleum corridors on wheelchairs and gurneys, was the last place I wanted to be.

As it turned out, the test didn't take long, and within an hour I was home again making myself lunch, looking forward to getting my work done, when the phone rang. It was my family doctor, calling to discuss the results of the sonogram. I remember thinking it unusual for him to get back to me so quickly; unless the test turns up some serious problem, doctors commonly send the results through the mail. "Sandy," he said, in what struck me a weary tone, "this is Doctor Walker. I'm afraid I have some bad news." I immediately recalled something my mother told me years ago, after my father's death from bone cancer. She told me how they had learned of the diagnosis when the doctor called to report the results of a routine lab test. She said that when they hung up the phone, they knew immediately that nothing would ever be the same, that their lives had been shattered beyond repair.

In my case, the sonogram taken only a few hours before had turned up images of a tumor the size of a golf ball, lodged deeply in the interior of my pancreas. Surgery was not an option. There were also spots in my liver that indicated the cancer had metastasized. I asked the doctor what I needed to do. "Find an oncologist," he bluntly replied. "Without immediate treatment you cannot expect to live more than a few months." The unimaginable had come to me like lightning from a clear blue sky.

The first thing I did was phone my wife at work. I told her the doctor had called with test results and that I'd like for her to leave work immediately so we could discuss what he said. She made the necessary arrangements, and before ten minutes had passed, I was there to pick her up. I couldn't find any words, though, so I simply drove. After a few minutes she whispered, "What is it, honey? What did he say?" I told her that I had been diagnosed with stage 4 pancreatic cancer—a bad one even as cancers go. That without medical attention I'd be dead within two or three months, that one way or another I most likely had little more than a year at best. Neither of us spoke, and after a long silence, she began to cry.

When we got home, we sat together and began processing what needed to be done, which turned out to be a lot of phone calls to various offices and clinics. We spent the remainder of the afternoon making some of those calls, which kept us occupied. But as evening approached and the sunlight faded into darkness, there was nothing to do other than sit together and cry. We went to bed early, holding each other close, declaring our mutual love, weeping at the meaningless suffering of the world and at what life had done to us, demolishing, so quickly and cruelly, all our dreams of a future together.

Anthony Lane recently wrote for an essay published by the *New Yorker*:

> In the cozier nooks of the well-furnished and relentlessly medicated West . . . we have told ourselves—or fooled ourselves—that life, far from hanging by a thread, is sitting comfortably, pouring itself a drink, putting on some Michael Bublé, and going nowhere in a hurry.[103]

But this was *not* me; I harbored no such ideas about life "sitting comfortably, going nowhere in a hurry." Quite the contrary. In the years previous to receiving this call from my doctor, I had worked as a volunteer for hospice, offering company to dying patients in the lonely, disinfected rooms where we house our elders. For eight of those years I had been teaching a class titled "Near Death Experience," in which we read books explaining what it means—both physically and psychologically—to die in contemporary America, and every student in the class served as a hospice volunteer. I had for years been an avid consumer of books on death and dying, everything from Sherwin Nuland's *How We Die*, with its unsparing, meticulous descriptions of the mayhem that rains down on the body in its final days (one of my friends called the book "death porn") to Atul Gawande's gentle, soothing voice in *Being Mortal* and Paul Kalanithi's heart-wrenching account of his own dying at age thirty-five, movingly narrated in *When Breath Becomes Air*. These and countless other more obscure titles. I read them all, to the point where my family routinely joked about my obsession with the literature of death.

They were right: I was obsessed with death. It was an obsession that found its roots in my undergraduate years, when I first encountered existentialist authors like Jean Paul Sartre and Albert Camus. The obsession matured throughout the decades of my long engagement with Buddhism, a tradition that tends, like many other religions, to see spiritual work as preparation for death. This is of course obvious in the case of the *Tibetan Book of the Dead*, but the message is communicated, one way or another, throughout Buddhist teachings, where meditations on death are commonplace. The years I had lived in India also contributed to my fascination. In contemporary America, we hide death; in India, death is everywhere visible. In Banaras, a city where I lived for years, corpses of animals lie in the streets alongside the occasional beggar who simply expired where he or she had been squatting with his dented aluminum bowl. Banaras is considered by many Hindus to be the ideal place to die. In the back alleyways leading to the Ganges River, there are hotels filled with emaciated men and women waiting to be taken up by the great god Shiva. Those not fortunate enough to die within city limits are brought there by relatives and carried through the streets on bamboo biers to be cremated on the banks of the river. As the pallbearers wind through the narrow alleys leading to Manikarnika—a concrete platform overlooking the river where the cremation fires burn night and day—they keep up a steady chant of *Rama nama satya hai!*—"The name of God is Truth!" In the neighborhood of Assi, I could hear these funeral processions from where I sat in my room, bent over my desk, studying or translating. Smoke from the cremation fires billows upward over the city and perfumes the air with the acrid smell of burning human flesh and hair. In those days, living far from "the cozier nooks of the well-furnished and relentlessly medicated West," I considered myself on familiar terms with death, just as I did on that day in January when my doctor called to deliver the "bad news." It struck me, then, that what I knew about the death of others had nothing to do with my own death. I was like a scholar knowing litanies of Buddhist doctrine but not being able to assimilate them existentially. This was a death far more real than anything I had encountered in books, Buddhist or otherwise, or when sitting with my hospice patients. This was a death suddenly pressing in on me from all sides, leading me down a blind alley that ended—or so it seems—with the loss of everything about my present self and world.

That call set in motion several days of frenetic activity as I phoned one specialist after another in an effort to set treatment in motion as quickly as possible. It was hard to focus on all the bureaucratic details, to talk with all the functionaries, only to be placed on hold, again and again, with the phone pressed to my ear, listening to some insipid music, the pain in my gut an ever-present reminder of what was at stake. But making these contacts, I discovered, was entirely my responsibility. No nurse or doctor or hospital bureaucrat was going to do it for me. I remember blurting out to one poor secretary, when she told me that none of the resident oncologists presently had any space in their schedule: *For you and the doctors this is just another day at work, another anonymous patient; but for me time is running out. I'm dying!* The poor woman was clearly flustered. After a moment of shocked silence, she promised, in a voice filled with urgency and compassion, to do whatever she could to help me find a doctor. There were also, during this first week, endless discussions with insurance providers. The problem was that I had not only to find a local oncologist but also to schedule an appointment with a specialist at Dana Farber, a state-of-the-art cancer treatment center four hours away in Boston where I could get a second opinion. This required clearance from my HMO, which in turn required jumping through one flaming hoop after another. Eventually I was granted permission to schedule the appointment, and my wife and I made the drive to Boston. I don't know what we expected or hoped for, perhaps some magical cure that only these elite, Harvard doctors could deliver. Instead, we were told only that the original diagnosis was correct, and the chemotherapy prescribed by my oncologist was the gold standard. The long drive to Boston turned out to be pointless.

In the following weeks I became a regular customer at the cancer clinic in our local hospital. I quickly learned to see my body as nothing more than an object to be pushed and prodded and trundled in and out of a succession of sterile, fluorescent-lit examination rooms, where "it" became the subject of detached, scientific analysis that had nothing to do with me as a person, with my delights and passions and disappointments, all those memories of my childhood, the years in India and graduate school. None of this was relevant because I was no longer a person; I had morphed into a diseased organ. This was war, and the doctors were fighting on my side, focused on a single task. The tumors must be forced to submit. I had a biopsy taken; the surgeon inserted a long needle through a spot just below my ribs, pushing it deep into the dark, intimate recesses above my abdomen. It was nothing short of a violent invasion, though you wouldn't know it, for everyone from the attending technicians to the surgeon seemed to be in an upbeat mood. When the needle reached my liver, the surgeon let it rest there for moment before piercing through the surprisingly resilient skin (a profoundly alien sensation) and setting his little blades twirling so as to extract a sample of tissue. During these first few weeks I also had a rubber bulb installed under the skin in my chest, connected via a tube to an artery in my neck. Since then this "port" has facilitated the insertion of a series of needles used to extract blood for lab tests or to pump into my bloodstream a biweekly cocktail of poisonous chemicals that will, theoretically, slow the growth of the tumors and so buy me a few more days or weeks among the living.

At the moment of this writing the chemo seems to be working, as there are indications that the tumors are shrinking. There is, however, no cure for stage 4 pancreatic cancer. It is a terminal diagnosis, though for the majority of patients the endgame can at least be postponed. With the proper chemotherapy the tumors will usually stop growing and begin withering away until they reach what the doctors call a "plateau." At some point, inevitably, the dying tumors will adapt to the chemo and begin swelling again. No one knows how long it will take before all this plays out; it could be a matter of days or weeks or months before the chemo no longer works. People with pancreatic cancer sometimes live as long as a year or even more. Such miracles are rare but not unheard of. Nevertheless, at some point the tumors almost certainly will start to swell and grow again, and chances are very great that this will come about in the not too distant future. In the meantime I must live with the biweekly chemo treatments.

The side effects of the lethal poisons being infused into my bloodstream are debilitating. I'm constantly fatigued, so much so that while sitting or lying down on the couch, I regularly slip into a sort of trance state defined by the slow, steady rhythm of my breathing. For as long as it lasts I am simply erased. Left with no purpose in mind, nothing whatsoever to think or do, I just sit quietly, wearied beyond belief but somehow at peace. Even my own dying no longer matters. The experience is similar to certain tranquil meditative states I've known. In this sense it is familiar, but in another way it's unlike any meditation I've done in the past. At those times there was always some trace of self that remained, but in these trance-like states I am swept away by a level of acceptance unprecedented in my experience. I may remain like this for only a few minutes, or for half an hour or more; it always comes as a blessing, a taste of something infinitely deeper. To leave this immense silence behind, to rise and stand and once again face the reality of my dying on other, more quotidian terms, then requires an immense effort. I shuffle from one room to the next like a stereotype of the old, sick man I have in fact become in only a few months.

The devastating weariness and its attendant symptoms, however, are only one side effect of chemotherapy. There are also problems with my sense of touch and taste. My tongue is now perpetually numb, buzzing and tingling with what feels like an electric current; my mouth coated with a foul, chemical taste. All food is, for me, tasteless cardboard. I force myself to eat because I must, in order not to lose another pound, in order to live another day. In the first month of chemotherapy, before they lightened my regimen, I could not put a spoonful of food in my mouth without retching. I have lost almost forty pounds, dropping from 186 to 148. As the fat leaves my body, my muscles begin to wither; my skin begins to wrinkle and sag. Crimson blotches spread over the back of my hands and wrists.

"This very body, the body of Buddha."

Along with its physical side effects, the treatment I'm now enduring has had other psychological or spiritual consequences. The tranquil states I just described appear to be one such consequence, not at all unpleasant. Another entirely unanticipated development, perhaps related to these "states," has also been enormously helpful in these otherwise dark times. The chemo—or the illness (it's impossible to know which)—is sapping me, day by day, of my allegiance to the ego's motives and concerns, motives and concerns that I now clearly see have defined me throughout my adult life. The ego's constant strategizing, its need to assert control and shape circumstances on its own terms, its delight in accomplishment and despair in defeat—all of this is increasingly remote from and irrelevant to my present situation. The Persian poet Rumi advises us to "hatch out the total helplessness inside,"[104] and that is what I'm doing, or what is being done to me. None of the ego's formidable powers has anything of value to offer me now; they are up against a power far beyond reckoning. Moreover, insofar as the ego's motives and concerns are bound up with the ego's insatiable thirst for more—more reading, more writing, more time with my family and friends, more *life*—they issue a promissory note that will never be cashed because I no longer have more time, even in my imagination. But this makes no difference to the ego; the ego keeps on churning out desires for *more* that make it hard to find peace with the future I no longer have. And yet, as the world slips through my fingers, becoming with the passing days ever more tenuous and insubstantial, everything about it has at the same time become frightfully precious, every tiny detail—the meadow in front of our house with its tall grass rippling in the breeze, the bright yellow buttercups and dusty blue forget-me-nots, the mournful song of the doves at twilight—is more vivid and compelling, more real, than ever before. It is just like my lucid dream experience: this new reality is unlike anything I could ever have imagined. It's as if the world is reaching out to me with the arms of a lover to draw me into itself, to erase all that I have been in the strength of its embrace.

Much of this may sound odd, or perhaps sad, to healthy people still immersed in worldly affairs and in their dreams and plans, hopes and expectations. I know this is true because not very long ago I was one of those people, confidently looking toward the future. I well knew, from my hospice work, my study of Buddhism, and all my other reading that I was in denial, but it was the sort of denial that all of us habitually indulge. For all I know we may need to live this way; to confront the truth squarely on its own terms may not be possible for anyone other than saints and buddhas. But for me things have changed. In facing my own imminent death, all the attitudes and techniques that I honed over the years in my search for the approval of others have become useless, or worse. The thread of imagination that connected me to the future has abruptly snapped, and in order to avoid sinking into despair at the devastating loss I face, I'm called upon to go beyond the ego into an unknown and forbidding territory: the realm of the non-future. In my inexorable physical decline, I move ever closer to the cottage of darkness, to the jaws of the Leviathan, to the nothingness that has been buried inside me and largely ignored all these years. In leading me inevitably toward this nothingness, my illness has become something very like what Tibetan Buddhists refer to as a "wrathful deity."

This wrathful deity has come to me out of compassion, to teach me hard lessons that all of us must eventually master. It is teaching me that the redemptive power of death will be revealed only when the ego with its demands for authority and control are swept away, along with the accompanying fear and dread, by an act of unequivocal self-surrender. As Laurens van der Post wrote, speaking to us out of his own experience of dying: "Gone at last are all the special pleadings, evasions and excuses that men use to blind themselves to the whole truth of themselves, discovering in the process their portion of the estate of aboriginal darkness to which they are the natural heirs and successors."[105]

The fact is, the ego relies in large part for its continued sovereignty on fantasies of future accomplishments or future pleasures. My ego thrives in conjuring up visions of retirement in the company of my wife and children, in looking forward to grandchildren, to continued social engagement with friends and colleagues, to continuing to work on a house I've been building in the hills outside of town. But my illness has revealed these hopes and anticipations for what they always were, the workings of an overactive imagination. The future was always a dream, and now the dream has ended, and I am left with the only thing I ever really had: the present. I live in a world where all the games of success and failure no longer have any appeal. As King Lear tells Cordelia,

> [We'll] hear poor rogues
> Talk of court news; and we'll talk with them too—
> Who loses and who wins; who's in and who's out—
> And take upon's the mystery of things,
> in a wall'd prison, packs and sects of great ones,
> That ebb and flow by th' moon.

Helen Luke has written about these lines: "Surely in all the world there could be no more profoundly beautiful, wise, and tender expression of the essence of old age, of the kind of life to which one may come in the last years if one has, like Lear, lived through and accepted all the passion and suffering, the darkness and the light, the beauty and horror of the world and of oneself."[106]

I wonder sometimes if the lesson this dying is teaching me is something like what Prince Gautama learned toward the end of his six years of asceticism, so perfectly depicted in that forbidding statue sitting in the museum in Lahore. It must have seemed to him that in abandoning his wife and child and his life in the palace he had lost forever all the things that previously made life worth living. The weight of this loss must have, for some time at least, not only deepened his meditations but also brought him to despair: it was certainly a catalyst for the extreme ascetic practices that almost killed him. What is of concern to me now—and what eventually seems to have concerned the prince, as well, judging from his later teaching—is not so much what has been lost but what "comes to birth only in a heart freed from preoccupation with the goals of the ego, however 'spiritual' or lofty these goals may be."[107] With the passing of the final weeks and days of my life, I am learning the hardest of lessons: to no longer want more than what I am given, and to allow what I have been given to guide me through the purifying flames of love and grief into the brilliant darkness of unknowing. Unlike Prince Gautama, though, I don't think I would ever have been desperate or vulnerable enough to open myself to these lessons were it not for my illness.

Dying casts a brutally honest light on all that has gone before, and of all the things that have gone before, the spiritual goals of the ego are especially pernicious. All the old attitudes that drove me to write and study and meditate appear, from my present perspective, as tainted with ego. Anything that has to do even peripherally with the ego's need to turn Buddhist teachings into a vehicle for self-improvement has now become a cause for pain, for the self and its unrelenting efforts to turn everything to its own purposes are precisely what keeps me from finding freedom inside this prison of necessity. I desperately require, now, only what is outside the realm of self-interest, outside the purview of "those packs and sects of great ones / That ebb and flow by th' moon." In my present anguish, I seek an innocence and simplicity that has nothing to do with the powers that have carried me this far. The compulsion to resist and revise the circumstances of my life, if only in the subtlest of ways, appears to me as nothing more than the perpetuation of a vain, arduous struggle pitting my will against insurmountable forces of nature, forces entirely outside my control that are pushing me into the black sack of death that is at once the source and conclusion of all our dreams of power and the "mystery of things" in which we live and move and have our being.

A week before he died, Thomas Merton wrote of an experience of deep peace that spontaneously seized his soul. He was standing in the garden of the Three Stone Buddhas in Sri Lanka when, without warning, he "was jerked clean out of the habitual half-tied vision of things." Merton went on in his diary to say that, overcome by this peace beyond understanding, he had "seen through every question without trying to discredit anyone or anything—*without refutation*—without establishing some other argument."[108] He was, in short, outside the realm of all those healthy souls still vying to occupy the center stage in whatever world matters most to them.

If I am to find a way to die in peace, it will only come through release from "the habitual half-tied vision of things" that is permeated with self-interest and delusion, with ideas of right and wrong, and this release will be found not simply in acceptance. I need something more than mere acceptance. I need to find my way to unconditional love, which is the only kind of love capable of embracing the immensity of my loss. In the absence of unconditional love, I face an unrelenting battle leading to certain defeat, a pointless, blind rage against the dying of the light of this ego-driven consciousness. My illness—this sliding into death that undermines my identity as an individual—compels me to search for a redemption consummated in what Helen Luke called "the joy which comes only when we no longer seek happiness."[109]

To go beyond happiness into joy means to be free of myself, and for that I need both unconditional love and its handmaiden—forgiveness. Forgiveness given freely by myself to myself, and as much as possible forgiveness offered to me by my family and friends. Forgiveness for the stream of self-deceptions necessitated by all those years of searching for happiness by judging and condemning and putting myself above others. I need also to forgive those others for the ways in which they have sought—most often without any conscious realization—to deceive me by making me into an instrument for the realization of their own selfish desires. Such forgiveness is impossible when my attention is absorbed by the machinations of an ego still bent on fueling its dreams of power. To truly forgive myself and others I must go beyond the ego and surrender to the darkness within, to the hidden, sacred miracle of life and death, and to the prison of necessity within which that miracle is made manifest to each of us in a different guise. This kind of total self-surrender entails precisely what the ego finds most difficult: patience in suffering; prayers for humility; delight and wonder at the simple enchantments of nature, in the telling of painful old stories, the sharing of memories now cast into the bright light of my dying.

Love in this context is not at all abstract, nor is grief. They are an all-consuming necessity. Between or within the two of them lies the realization, or belated acknowledgment, that I am dependent on others for my very existence and for whatever meaning and value I have managed to discover in seventy years of living. In other words, what I most need now is all that is *not* me.

Helen Luke writes, "There is no private salvation; exchange with the other is the door to the final awareness of the unity of all in the love which is the dance of creation."[110] I am now, more than ever before, aware of just how inextricably interwoven we are, how we carry within us the people and places we love and also all that we judge and reject and fear. Over the span of a long life, the weight of these judgments and fears becomes a dreadful burden. My adult persona, forever alone and in thrall to its self-centered needs and desires, forever rebounding between what is acceptable and what is not, will never allow me to live out these final days in peace, much less to face death with equanimity. For that I need a renewed innocence and simplicity, one that is capable of accepting the love and forgiveness and simple kindness of my family and friends and capable, as well, of offering love and forgiveness and kindness in return. In order to live what is left of my life and die in peace, the wrathful deity of death is teaching me to give myself over to the human community and to a felt kinship with the nonhuman world, a world to which I have always belonged while never fully appreciating the significance of that belonging, a world where this failing body of mine is, like all bodies, a tiny, fleeting shadow in the immensity of creation. In only a few months the gestalt has shifted, and after a lifetime of study and practice of Buddhism, I am only now learning, here in this prison of necessity, to release my grip on life and so to love life as it is, in all its beauty and horror, to give myself over to the embrace of those infinite others, human and nonhuman—the earth in which we are rooted, teaming with beetles and grubs and worms, the grass and flowers and trees, the robin building a nest outside my window, the hawk circling high overhead, the clouds, wind, rain, and sun—all of whom have nourished and sustained me throughout this long journey home. They are in me, and I am in them. We are inseparable.

For all flesh is as grass, and all the glory of man as the flower of grass. The grass withereth, and flower thereof falleth away.

Epilogue

SANDY DIED ON JULY 19, 2020, at 1:45 p.m. It was an entirely quiet passing. He simply let go.

In his final days, Sandy often asked his wife Liz to read to him. The poem "Drive" that began this book was one of his favorites.

Sandy would recite the following version of the *metta* prayer during his meditation sessions and at the end of his classes in which students would meditate. It is his wish for all of us.

May I be well.
May I be content and at peace.

May my mother and father be well.
May they be content and at peace.

May my family be well.
May they be content and at peace.

May my friends be well.
May they be content and at peace.

May all those who are strangers to me be well.
May they be content and at peace.

May my enemies be well.
May they be content and at peace.

May the earth and all living beings be well.
May we be content and at peace.

Notes

The following notes amplify or deepen points made in the body of the text. If toggling back and forth between the notes and the essays becomes a distraction, consider a first reading without consulting them.

1. In adopting this hermeneutical approach, I find myself in accord with the perspective of Longchenpa, the renowned Tibetan Dzogchen visionary, as it is characterized by David Higgins. According to Higgins, Longchenpa's interpretation of the Mahayana philosopher Nagarjuna "provides a transition point from the propositional truths of representational thinking to the disclosive truth of existential understanding . . . What is at issue in this Mantrayana-oriented reintepretation of 'truth' is something akin to the Heideggerian distinction between *truth as correspondence,* the agreement (confirmation or disconfirmation) between propositions and states of affairs, and a more elementary form of *truth as disclosure*, which is simply the *display* of a state of affairs, and therefore the condition of possibility of propositional truth. For Longchenpa, the shift in perspective concerning truth coincides with the transition from representational thinking to primordial knowing. From a disclosive standpoint, 'emptiness' is not in the first instance a deductively formulated account of a state of affairs but describes the prepredicative display of a state of affairs before its being channeled through the categories of representational thinking and reified as this or that" (Higgins 2013, 114–15 [I have altered his spelling Klongchenpa to the phonetic Longchenpa]).
2. It seems to me that any form of logical positivism—with its principled, strident rejection of anything that smacks of mysticism and its corresponding commitment to the search for "objective truth"—is uniquely unsuited to serve as a hermeneutical guide toward interpretation of Buddhist literature, which is in its methods and goals either explicitly or implicitly devoted to a strictly

soteriological purpose. In this regard I am an outlier in the academic world of Buddhist studies, where "Buddhist philosophy" is nowadays overwhelmingly viewed through the lens of the secular, positivistic methods and goals of Anglo-American analytic philosophy, an enterprise that has been characterized by Scott Soames as philosophy that "aims at truth and knowledge, as opposed to moral or spiritual improvement." According to Soames, "the goal in analytic philosophy is to discover what is true, not to provide a useful recipe for living one's life" (Soames 2003, xiii–xvii). Arthur Danto sums up the extent to which this model of philosophy and its ideal of "objective truth" has been adopted by his peers: "I don't know whether, aside from etymology, wisdom especially figures in the concept of philosophy, at least among philosophers themselves, few of whom, in my fairly wide acquaintanceship, especially covet the epithet 'wise,' or even count wisdom as something they especially love. Philosophers love cleverness, acuity, fertility in inventing novel arguments, and ingenuity in finding surprising counter-examples. At least since the professionalization of the discipline in the 20th century, these have been what philosophers particularly admire in other philosophers" (Danto 2012). I have attempted to engage and critique this approach to Buddhist texts in my academic publications. That is not, however, my current project.

3. On this, see George Lakoff and Mark Johnson: "We found that . . . the dominant views on meaning in Western philosophy and linguistics are inadequate—that 'meaning' in these traditions has very little to do with what people find meaningful in their lives . . . The problem [is] not one of extending or patching up some existing theory of meaning but of revising central assumptions in the Western philosophical tradition. In particular, this meant rejecting the possibility of any objective or absolute truth and a host of related assumptions. It also meant supplying an alternative account in which human experience and understanding, rather than objective truth, played the central role." The alternative account they develop—from which I take my lead—views human experience as the principal determining factor of philosophical truth, a truth that is necessarily metaphorical rather than referential or literal: "We have found . . . that metaphor is pervasive in everyday life, not just in language but in thought and action. Our ordinary conceptual system, in terms of which we both think and act, is fundamentally metaphorical in nature . . . If we are right in suggesting that our conceptual system is largely metaphorical, then the way we think, what we experience, and what we do every day is very much a matter of metaphor" (Lakoff and Johnson 1980, ix–x, 4). Lakoff and Johnson's views are echoed by Denys Turner in his discussion of medieval Christian theology: "*nothing* invisible is capable of being described or known otherwise than in and through the representations of the visible . . . And the constraint is quite general onto-

logically: it is because of the way the world is that theological method is constrained to work by means of the symbolic; it is not because of some imperative of theological method that we need to see the world in that way. The world's character of being created means that it *is* symbol, representation, image. That is its reality and its truth" (Turner 1995, 104).

4. I am certainly not the first to find fruitful parallels between apophatic Christian mysticism and its Buddhist counterpart; there is an extensive literature on the subject. As someone who has spent his professional life in academia, I'm nevertheless acutely aware that there are many people who for many good reasons are highly skeptical of anything that smacks of perennialism. Still, I find myself sympathetic with David Bentley Hart when he points out that "no one really acquainted with the metaphysical and spiritual claims of the major theistic faiths can fail to notice that on a host of fundamental philosophical issues, and especially on the issue of how divine transcendence should be understood, the areas of accord are quite vast" (Hart 2013, 4). And I find myself in agreement as well with his suggestion that the conception of God offered by classical theologians across many traditions is—allowing for historical and circumstantial variations—strikingly similar to early Buddhist conceptions of nirvana as the unconditioned, to later Mahayana Buddhist formulations of buddha nature, and to Tibetan Dzogchen teachings on open awareness. However, what attracts me in this context to the literature of medieval Christian mysticism is not only its striking parallels with elements of Buddhist soteriology but also, and primarily, its boundless stock of tropes, a rich metaphorical language that is capable, on occasion, of opening up fresh avenues for interpretation of Buddhist thought and practice.
5. Hamilton 2016, 23.
6. Nussbaum 1986, xliii.
7. Ecclesiastes 1:9.
8. Translated in Olivelle 2008.
9. This passage is found in most editions of the Anglican *Book of Common Prayer* in the section dealing with burial rites. See too Job 14:1–2.
10. Hart 2013, 11.
11. Hamilton 2014, 9.
12. Excerpted from "Notice," by Steve Kowit (1994).
13. Excerpted from "The Well of Grief," by David Whyte (1997).
14. Becker 1973, 282–83.
15. Eliot 1978, 126.
16. Carey 2007.
17. Merton 1948, 82–83.
18. See Jacobs 1997, 17–30, for citations from "The Monkey's Paw."

19. Matthew 6:10.
20. Eagleton, "Commentary," in Felski 2008, 339.
21. Hamilton 2016, 37.
22. Turner 1995, 183–84.
23. The title of this chapter is borrowed from a line in Mary Oliver's poem "When Death Comes" (Oliver 1992, 10–11).
24. Shakespeare, *As You Like It*, act 2, scene 7. For this and the following citations from Jaques's monologue on the seven ages of man, see Shakespeare 2005.
25. Shakespeare, *As You Like It*, act 2, scene 7.
26. Schneider 2019.
27. Robinson 2010, 110–11.
28. The Christian mystic Meister Eckhart held a remarkably similar view of the self: "[T]here is something which is above the created being of the soul and which is untouched by any createdness, which is to say *nothingness* . . . It is akin to the divine nature, it is united in itself, it has nothing in common with anything at all . . . It is a strange land and a desert, and it is more without a name than nameable, more unknown than knowable" (translated from the German in Davies 1988, 50).
29. Salinger 1991, 65.
30. Holub 1997, 490.
31. Shakespeare, *As You Like It*, act 2, scene 7.
32. Nisargadatta Maharaj 1973, 442.
33. Berry 2001, 103.
34. Kaplan 1999, 37.
35. Seife 2000, 2.
36. Seife 2000, 39.
37. Vaidya 1960c, 97. All translations from Vaidya's editions are by the author.
38. Vaidya 1960a, 217.
39. Vaidya 1960a, 96.
40. Vaidya 1960c, 84.
41. Vaidya 1960c, 86.
42. Vaidya 1960c, 79.
43. Vaidya 1960c, 97.
44. Vaidya 1960a, 96.
45. Kaplan 1999, 59–60. I've altered Kaplan's spelling of *shunya* to conform with the spelling I've adopted throughout this chapter.
46. See Kaplan 1999, 60.
47. Vaidya 1960c, 89. The Sanskrit differs a bit from my English adaptation, which aims to capture the poetic spirit of the original text.
48. Hawking 2018, 28–29. The whole of chapter 2 in Hawking's book offers a fas-

cinating commentary on and contrast with our present discussion. He is, as William James remarked about Freud, "in the grip of a fixed idea."

49. Wills 1976, vol. 1, 239–40.
50. Hart 2013, 64. For an engaging discussion of the historical origins and development of this metaphor of the cosmos as a mindless machine, see Hart 2013, 46–84: "Pictures of the World." Denys Turner does a nice job of summing it up: "'Modernity,' at least as a seventeenth-century modern such as Thomas Hobbes saw it, supplanted [the medieval] view of the world as a web of symbolic representations with the view of the world as a mechanical system of interacting efficient causes" (Turner 1995, 104). Notice, however, that modernity did not escape the medieval world view; it merely ceased to see its own favored metaphor *as* a metaphor.
51. Spearing 2001, 4.
52. Spearing 2001, 94.
53. Excerpted from "This Only," by Czeslaw Milosz (1988, 460).
54. I'm indebted to Seife 2000, 85–86, for some of the content of this paragraph and for his image of the accompanying illustration.
55. Higgins 2013, 84. Augustine, in his *Confessions*, refers to this as "*acies mentis*, the 'cutting edge' of the mind, the place 'in' it which overlaps with the eternal Light it is in" (Turner 1995, 99).
56. Thanks to Sam Huntington for this wonderful drawing, and to Douglas Harding for the inspiration to depict first-person experience from this particular visual perspective. From among Harding's many publications, his first book—*On Having No Head* (1961)—remains, in my view, the definitive statement of his unique vision.
57. It's difficult not to find an intriguing parallel in Moses's encounter with God on Mount Sinai, which was eventually taken up by medieval theologians and incorporated into the apophatic discourse that characterized much of the medieval Christian mystical tradition. According to the biblical account in Exodus 33:18–23, God descended on the mountain in an incandescent blaze of lightning and fire completely engulfed by a thick cloud of smoke: "Moses said, 'Please show me your glory.' And [Yahweh] said, 'I will make all my goodness pass before you and will proclaim before you my name . . . and I will be gracious to whom I will be gracious, and will show mercy on whom I will show mercy. But,' he said, 'you cannot see my face, for man shall not see me and live.' And the Lord said, 'Behold, there is a place by me where you shall stand on the rock, and while my glory passes by I will put you in a cleft of the rock, and I will cover you with my hand until I have passed by. Then I will take away my hand, and you shall see my back, but my face shall not be seen.'" Gregory of Nyssa comments: "For leaving behind everything that is observed, not only what sense comprehends but also what the intelligence thinks it sees, [the mind] keeps

on penetrating deeper until by the intelligence's yearning for understanding it gains access to the invisible and incomprehensible, and there it sees God. This is the true knowledge of what is sought; this is the seeing that consists in not seeing, because that which is sought transcends all knowledge, being separated on all sides by incomprehensibility as by a kind of darkness" (Malherbe and Ferguson 1978, 94–95). And Bonaventure: "Thus our mind, accustomed as it is to the opaqueness in beings and the phantasms of visible things, appears to be seeing nothing when it gazes upon the light of the highest being. It cannot understand that this very darkness is the supreme illumination of our mind, just as when the eye sees pure light, it seems to be seeing nothing" (Cousins 1978, fructus 5, section 4).

58. Hart 2013, 93. In this context, see also Turner's discussion of the paradox of Augustine's encounter with God: "The paradox is, then, that there, where God is most intimately and 'subjectively' interior to us, our inwardness turns out beyond itself towards the eternal and boundless objectivity of Truth" (Turner 1995, 69).
59. Turner 1995, 73.
60. *Karuna* is commonly translated as "compassion," but that choice is problematic. The Greek word *agape* is closer to the mark, especially as it is used in the expression "God is love," found in 1 John 4:8 and 4:16. There it refers to a particular sacramental, self-sacrificing form of love extended by God to humans and by humans both to God and to each other and, ultimately, to all of creation. In any case, as a translation of *karuna*, "love" is a force that takes the mind beyond language and conceptual thought.
61. Tolstoy 1959, 71.
62. Tolstoy 1959, 72.
63. Tolstoy 1959, 72–73.
64. Brombert 2013, 13.
65. Tolstoy 1959, 73.
66. Robinson 2010, 32.
67. Robinson 2010, 32.
68. Hart 2013, 4 and 197.
69. Brombert 2013, 23.
70. Nisargadatta Maharaj 1973, 269.
71. Armbrecht 2009, 214.
72. Dostoyevsky 1969, 211.
73. Rich 1986, 100.
74. Miles 1986, 84.
75. As to whether this kind of altruism is "entirely beyond our imagining," it is worth noting that there has been and continues to be a raging debate among

Western philosophers about the very possibility of altruism. For a good review of the principal players in this debate and the issues felt to be at stake, see chapter 2 in Robinson 2010, "The Strange History of Altruism."

76. Green and McCreery 1994, 65 and 67.
77. Vaidya 1960d, 64.
78. Mark 4:12.
79. Issa 1997, xv.
80. Excerpted from "Oceans," by Juan Ramón Jiménez, reprinted in Housden 2003, 35.
81. Johnston 2009, 124.
82. Here's something interesting: I recently came across a study suggesting that we don't necessarily know whether we're awake or asleep. That is to say, when we are lying in bed anxiously waiting to fall asleep, frustrated that sleep will not come, we may in fact *already* be asleep and only dreaming we are awake. So the author of the study—a clinical psychologist who works with patients suffering from insomnia—recommends that you simply lie still in bed, under the covers, in the dark, quiet room, with your eyes closed, *as if* you were asleep. That way, if you're not presently sleeping, chances are much greater that you soon will be. And even if you don't eventually fall asleep, by simply remaining still, with your eyes closed, you'll get a lot of the benefits of rest. The point is: you cannot know whether you are awake or asleep, so just relax.
83. That is: "There is no suffering, no origin, no cessation, no spiritual path. There is no wisdom. There is nothing to attain" (Vaidya 1960c, 97). I cited this same line above in the chapter "Absence and Presence."
84. *Fundamental Verses on the Middle Way* 25.19 (Vaidya 1960b, 234). For a rigorous philological account of Nagarjuna's perspective on this issue, through the eyes of his most famous classical commentator, see MacDonald 2009, 145–46 *et passim*: "The Madhyamaka *nirvāṇa* is the world itself—in its innate and eternal state of peaceful non-arising. As the true nature of the world and the phenomena constituting it, it is not even, as the other school's *nirvāṇa* is, something to be *attained* through escape from the world, for it is already ontologically anticipated in things themselves and merely requires insight into this fact. The old opposition between *nirvāṇa* and *saṃsāra* is replaced in Madhaymaka with an identification of *nirvāṇa* and *saṃsāra*, or rather with an identification of *nirvāṇa* and the true nature of *saṃsāra*. . . . It is against this larger background the seemingly paradoxical statements found in Madhyamaka texts as well as in Prajñāpāramitā and Mahāyāna literature in general which state that the *yogin* sees the ultimate by not-seeing, or that 'non-seeing is seeing' are to be understood. . . . Candrakīrti also defines *nirvāṇa* via the seeming paradox: he asserts that the thorough knowing of the non-arising of a real nature of existence which

occurs by way of non thorough-knowing, is said to be *nirvāṇa*." This is one place where the apophatic discourse of Buddhist Madhyamaka and that of Christian medieval theology overlap in a basic and striking way, opening the possibility of original and mutually fructifying interpretative strategies for both traditions.

85. Turner 1995, 72.
86. Higgins 2013, 266.
87. Abram 2010, 76.
88. *Anirvāṇaṃ hi nirvāṇaṃ lokanāthena deśitaṃ / ākāśena kṛto grantir ākāśenaiva mocitaḥ*. For a full study of the verse, including references to the original texts where it appears, see Apple 2016.
89. See Deguchi, Garfield, and Priest 2013 for the citation in its full context.
90. By "nothing" I of course mean "zero-ness" (*shunya-ta*). I'm fully aware of how preposterous it must appear to analytic philosophers for me to seriously suggest that Nagarjuna's arguments could be construed as a sort of theatrical performance. For the moment, the best I can do is to refer them back to the citation from Higgins 2013 in note 1 and to Lakoff and Johnson 1980, 5–6: "Our conventional ways of talking about arguments pre-suppose a metaphor we are hardly ever conscious of. The metaphor is not merely in the words we use—it is in our very concept of an argument. The language of argument is not poetic, fanciful, or rhetorical; it is literal. We talk about arguments that way because we conceive of them that way—and we act according to the way we conceive of things." Nagarjuna unequivocally states that he has no view or proposition to assert or defend; to take this statement as itself a proposition—as logicians feel compelled to do—engenders an apparent paradox that must then be explained. In projecting our preferred metaphor onto his text, they create a whole set of problems that they then feel compelled to solve but that are insolvable within the terms dictated by their conception of what constitutes legitimate philosophical argumentation.

    But how much can we really know about how readers in ancient India viewed Nagarjuna's arguments, under what metaphor they organized their understanding of the meaning and purpose of philosophical argumentation? What we do know is that the ultimate purpose of Nagarjuna's writing was soteriological; he makes that point repeatedly. I want to suggest, following Lakoff and Johnson's provocative lead, that there is an alternative way of understanding Nagarjuna that avoids both the perceived problems in his claim that he has no view or proposition and their various logical solutions: "Try to imagine a culture where arguments are not viewed in terms of war, where no one wins or loses, where there is no sense of attacking or defending, gaining or losing ground. Imagine a culture where an argument is viewed as a dance, the participants are seen as performers, and the goal is to perform in a balanced and aesthetically pleasing way" (Lakoff and Johnson 1980, 4–5). Try for a moment, then—as a thought experiment—to imagine that in Nagarjuna's writing, the concerns of Buddhist soteriology fundamentally shape the way argumentation was conceived by his ancient Indian Buddhist readers, such that the point of arguing was not to defend one's own view against the view of another but rather to use language as a means to paint a particular picture of the world—that is, to *show* his readers how the world appears to a buddha or bodhisattva. Argumentation in this sense is conceived as kind of ritual performance intended not to encourage readers to proceed from a premise or proposition to a literal, logically structured conclusion—to adopt, that is, a novel belief, conviction, or view in place of a belief, conviction, or view previously held; instead, it is intended to move readers, intellectually and emotionally, toward a new aesthetic that allows them to let go of the need to hold any particular view and so to enter into a condition of profound *un*knowing that is characteristic of Buddhist awakening. For an interesting discussion of how the Tibetan philosopher Gorampa developed a version of this reading in his understanding of the *tetralemma*—Nagarjuna's preeminent "logical tool"—see Kassor 2013.

One might also consult the preface to Klein and Wangyal 2006 for an insightful discussion of how logical discourse and literary, poetic readings of such discourse blend imperceptibly in Tibetan Buddhist texts. What Klein has to say about those texts is, in my view, equally applicable to Nagarjuna: "To best take its measure, we must recognize the work for what it is: first, a complex philosophical treatise that deploys reasoned argumentation; second, an artful work of literature that makes its meaning through image, metaphor, and multitudinous manipulations of the hidden currents and unintended disclosures that run through all writing" (Klein and Wangyal 2006, xi). There is no a priori reason not to read Nagarjuna from this point of view, and there is much to be gained. All that is required is to allow oneself to try, to open up to a new and unfamiliar perspective on the relation between reason and metaphor. Both I and various analytic philosophers are working within the community of academic philosophers to proselytize Nagarjuna; the difference between us is that the latter seek to accomplish this goal by reading Nagarjuna through an established and respectable lens, whereas I would prefer to challenge Western models with a perspective that calls into question our assumptions of what philosophy is or can be.

91. Mitchell 1993, 98.

92. See, for example, Denys Turner on the theology of Christian apophatic mysticism and its use of the "self-subverting utterance": "We could say that the predicament for theology is rather like that of the verbose teacher, who in shame at having talked too much in class, lapses into an embarrassed silence. Good

theology . . . has the same outcome, for it leads to that silence that is found only on the other side of linguistic embarrassment. *But that embarrassment has to be procured*, and to reach that point . . . it is necessary for theology to talk too much" (Turner 1995, 22–23 [emphasis added]). What is procured in this abundance of language "is not some intelligible *synthesis* of affirmation and negation; it is rather the collapse of our affirmation and denials into disorder, which we can only express, *a fortiori*, in bits of collapsed, disordered language . . . And that is what the 'self-subverting' utterance is, a bit of disordered language" (Turner 1995, 22). For Turner, there is no such thing as apophatic language per se; the apophatic is realized when language "breaks down," revealing the silence that lies hidden all around its perimeter (Turner 1995, 150).

93. Excerpted from "The Man Watching," by Rainer Maria Rilke (1981).
94. Steinthall 1982, 80–81.
95. Steinthall 1982, 81.
96. See Crane 2005, 223–29, for citations from "Football."
97. Nietzsche 1974, 273–74, book 4, no. 341.
98. James 1982, 474.
99. Higgins 2013, 262.
100. See Turner 1995, 182, for an interesting parallel to this idea of "desire turning back on itself" in the theology of the thirteenth-century German mystic Meister Eckhart. Eckhart spoke of detachment in the following terms: "To say that someone is detached is to say this: that her desire and God's will are identical. She would then not desire God out of any motivation, or for any reason or with any intention, because any of those can govern her desire only in so far as it is *not* identical with God's will. In the nothingness of detachment there is nothing in my desire which answers the question why I should love God, any more than there can be in God any reason why God should love God. To be detached is to live 'without a why.' It is to love God with an uncreated, undifferentiated love. It is not to be a being without desire." For Eckhart, "God's will" is simply what is given in the joys and sorrows of our day-to-day life.
101. These lines are excerpted from Hakuin's "Song of Zazen" as they appear in the standard English translation used in the liturgy manuals of most American Rinzai Zen centers. Hakuin Ekakku (1686–1769) was one of the most influential figures in the Japanese Rinzai Zen tradition.
102. Excerpted from "Kindness," by Naomi Shihab Nye (1995, 42–43).
103. Lane 2020, 62.
104. From "Prayer Is an Egg," in Barks, 2001, 104.
105. Van der Post 1982, 73.
106. Luke 1987, 25–26.
107. Luke 1987, 29.

108. Merton 1975, 48.
109. Luke 1987, 102.
110. Luke 1987, 61.

Bibliography

Abram, David. 2010. *Becoming Animal: An Earthly Cosmology*. New York: Pantheon Books.

Apple, James. 2016. "'The Knot Tied with Space': Note on a Previously Unidentified Stanza in Buddhist Literature and Its Citation." *Indian International Journal of Buddhist Studies* 17: 167–202.

Armbrecht, Ann. 2009. *Thin Places: A Pilgrimage Home*. New York: Columbia University Press.

Barks, Coleman, trans. 2001. *The Soul of Rumi: A New Collection of Ecstatic Poems.* San Francisco: HarperCollins.

Becker, Ernest. 1973. *The Denial of Death*. New York: Free Press.

Berry, Wendell. 2001. *Life Is a Miracle: An Essay against Modern Superstition*. Seattle: Counterpoint.

Brombert, Victor. 2013. *Musings on Mortality: From Tolstoy to Primo Levi*. Chicago: University of Chicago Press.

Carey, Benedict. 2007. "Denial Makes the World Go Round." *New York Times* (November 20).

Cousins, Ewart, trans. 1978. *Bonaventure: The Soul's Journey into God, The Tree of Life, The Life of St. Francis.* New York: Paulist Press.

Crane, Elizabeth. 2005. *All This Heavenly Glory*. New York: Little, Brown.

Danto, Arthur. 2012. "Letter to Posterity." *American Scholar* (September 4). https://theamericanscholar.org/letter-to-posterity/

Davies, Oliver. 1988. *God Within: The Mystical Tradition of Northern Europe*. New York: Paulist Press.

Deguchi, Yasuo, Jay Garfield, and Graham Priest. 2013. "Those Concepts Proliferate Everywhere: A Response to Constance Kassor." *Philosophy East and West* 63.3: 411–16.

Dostoevsky, Fyodor. 1969. "The Dream of a Ridiculous Man." In *From Karamzin to Bunin: An Anthology of Russian Short Stories*, translated by Carl R. Proffer. Bloomington: Indiana University Press.

Eliot, T. S. 1978 [1950]. *The Cocktail Party*. New York and London: Harcourt Brace Jovanovich.

Felski, Rita, ed. 2008. *Rethinking Tragedy*. Baltimore: Johns Hopkins University Press.

Green, Celia, and Charles McCreery. 1994. *Lucid Dreaming: The Paradox of Consciousness during Sleep*. New York: Routledge.

Hamilton, Christopher. 2014. *How to Deal with Adversity*. London: Macmillan.

Hamilton, Christopher. 2016. *A Philosophy of Tragedy*. London: Reaktion.

Harding, Douglas. 1961. *On Having No Head: Zen and the Rediscovery of the Obvious*. London: Arkana.

Hart, David Bentley. 2013. *The Experience of God: Being, Consciousness, Bliss*. New Haven, CT: Yale University Press.

Hawking, Stephen. 2018. *Brief Answers to the Big Questions*. New York: Bantam.

Higgins, David. 2013. *The Philosophical Foundations of Classical Rdzogs Chen in Tibet: Investigating the Distinction between the Dualistic Mind (sems) and Primordial Knowing (ye shes)*. Vienna: Arbeitskreis für Tibetische und Buddhistische Studien, Universität Wien.

Holub, Miroslav. 1997. "Shedding Life." In *Eyewitnesses to Science*, edited by John Carey, 488–91. Cambridge, MA: Harvard University Press.

Housden, Roger. 2003. *Risking Everything: 110 Poems of Love and Revelation*. New York: Harmony Books.

Issa, Kobayashi. 1997. *The Spring of My Life: And Selected Haiku*. Translated by Sam Hamill. Boston: Shambhala Publications.

Jacobs, W. W. 1997. *The Monkey's Paw and Other Tales of Mystery and the Macabre*. Chicago: Academy Chicago Publishers.

James, William. 1982 [1902]. *The Varieties of Religious Experience.* New York: Penguin Classics.

Johnston, Mark. 2009. *Saving God: Religion after Idolatry*. Princeton, NJ: Princeton University Press.

Kaplan, Robert. 1999. *The Nothing That Is: A Natural History of Zero*. New York: Oxford University Press.

Kassor, Constance. 2013. "Is Gorampa's 'Freedom from Conceptual Proliferations' Dialetheist?" *Philosophy East and West* 63.3: 399–410.

Klein, Anne, and Geshe Tenzin Wangyal Rinpoche. 2006. *Unbounded Wholeness: Dzogchen, Bon, and the Logic of the Nonconceptual.* Oxford: Oxford University Press.

Kowit, Steve. 1994. *Mysteries of the Body*. Olean, NY: Uroboros.

Lakoff, George, and Mark Johnson. 1980. *Metaphors We Live By*. Chicago: University of Chicago Press.

Lane, Anthony. 2020. "A Bug's Life." *New Yorker* (May 25): 57–62.

Luke, Helen. 1987. *Old Age: Journey into Simplicity.* New York: Bell Tower.

MacDonald, Anne. 2009. "Knowing Nothing: Candrakīrti and Yogic Perception." In *Yogic Perception, Meditation and Altered States of Consciousness*, edited by Eli Franco and Dagmar Eigner, 133–68. Vienna: Austrian Academy of Sciences Press.

Malherbe, Abraham J., and Everett Ferguson, trans. 1978. *Gregory of Nyssa: The Life of Moses.* New York: Paulist Press.

Merton, Thomas. 1948. *The Seven Storey Mountain.* New York: Harcourt Brace.

Merton, Thomas. 1975. *The Asian Journal.* New York: New Directions.

Miles, Sian, ed. 1986. *Simone Weil: An Anthology.* New York: Weidenfeld & Nicolson, 1986.

Milosz, Czeslaw. 1988. *Collected Poems, 1931–1987*. Translated by Robert Hass. New York: HarperCollins.

Mitchell, Stephen, ed. 1993. *The Enlightened Heart: An Anthology of Sacred Poetry*. New York: HarperPerennial.

Nietzsche, Friedrich. 1974. *The Gay Science.* Translated by Walter Kaufman. New York: Vintage Books.

Nisargadatta Maharaj. 1973. *I Am That*. Durham, NC: Acorn Press.

Nussbaum, Martha. 1986. *The Fragility of Goodness: Luck and Ethics in Greek Tragedy and Philosophy*. Cambridge: Cambridge University Press.

Nye, Naomi Shihab. 1995. *Words under the Words: Selected Poems*. Portland, OR: Far Corner Books.

Oldfather, W. A., trans. 1925–28. *Epictetus: The Discourses as Reported by Arrian, the Manual, and Fragments*. 2 vols. Loeb Classical Library. Cambridge, MA: Harvard University Press.

Olivelle, Patrick, trans. 2008. *Life of the Buddha by Ashvaghosha*. New York: New York University Press and JJC Foundation.

Rich, Adrienne. 1986. *Your Native Land, Your Life*. New York: W. W. Norton.

Rilke, Rainer Maria. 1981. *Selected Poems by Rainer Maria Rilke*. Translated by Robert Bly. New York: Harper and Row.

Robinson, Marilynne. 2010. *Absence of Mind: The Dispelling of Inwardness from the Modern Myth of the Self*. New Haven, CT: Yale University Press.

Salinger, J. D. 1991. *Franny and Zooey*. New York: Little, Brown.

Schneider, Susan. 2019. "Should You Add a Microchip to Your Brain?" *New York Times* (June 10).

Seife, Charlies. 2000. *Zero: The Biography of a Dangerous Idea*. New York: Penguin.

Shakespeare, William. 2005. *The Oxford Shakespeare: The Complete Works*. 2nd ed. Oxford: Oxford University Press.

Soames, Scott. 2003. *Philosophical Analysis in the Twentieth Century*. Vol. 1, *The Dawn of Analysis*. Princeton, NJ: Princeton University Press.

Spearing, A. C., trans. 2001. *The Cloud of Unknowing and Other Works*. New York: Penguin.

Steinthal, Paul, ed. 1982 [1885]. *Udāna*. London: Pali Text Society.

Tolstoy, Leo. 1959. *Ivan Ilyich, Hadji Murad, and Other Stories*. Translated by Louise and Aylmer Maude. London: Oxford University Press.

Turner, Denys. 1995. *The Darkness of God: Negativity in Christian Mysticism*. Cambridge: Cambridge University Press.

Vaidya, P. L., ed. 1960a. *Aṣṭasāhasrikāprajñāpāramitā*. Buddhist Sanskrit Texts 4. Darbhanga, India: Mithila Institute of Postgraduate Studies and Research in Sanskrit Learning.

Vaidya, P. L., ed. 1960b. *Madhyamakaśāstra of Nāgārjuna with the Commentary Prasannapadā by Candrakīrti*. Buddhist Sanskrit Texts 10. Darbhanga, India: Mithila Institute of Postgraduate Studies and Research in Sanskrit Learning.

Vaidya, P. L., ed. 1960c. *Mahāyāna-Sūtra-Saṃgraha, Part 1*. Buddhist Sanskrit Texts 17. Darbhanga, India: Mithila Institute of Postgraduate Studies and Research in Sanskrit Learning.

Vaidya, P. L., ed. 1960d. *Saddharmalaṅkāvatārasūtra*. Buddhist Sanskrit Texts 3. Darbhanga, India: Mithila Institute of Postgraduate Studies and Research in Sanskrit Learning.

Van der Post, Laurens. 1982. *Yet Being Someone Other*. London: Hogarth Prcss.

Vredeman de Vries, Jan. 1968 [1604]. *Perspective*. With a new introduction by Adolf K. Placzek. New York: Dover Publications.

Whyte, David. 1997. *The House of Belonging*. Langley, WA: Many Rivers Press.

Wills, Arthur, trans. 1976. *The Notebooks of Simone Weil*. 2 vols. London: Routledge and Kegan Paul.

Index

About the Author

C. W. "Sandy" Huntington Jr. was born February 24, 1949, and grew up in East Lansing, Michigan, walking distance from Michigan State University, where he later attended college. He earned his PhD in Asian Languages and Cultures at the University of Michigan under the guidance of Luis Gómez, training in Sanskrit with Madhav Deshpande and then, while living in India (1976–79), with Ambika Datta Upadhyaya and Ram Shankar Tripathi. Sandy would return to India, especially Banaras, many times during his life; for him it was a second home.

Sandy first taught at Antioch College's Buddhist Studies in India program, then at the University of Michigan and Denison College, before joining the faculty at Hartwick College in Oneonta, New York. There he inspired undergraduates for more than two decades, receiving numerous awards for teaching.

As a scholar, Sandy urged his colleagues in Buddhist philosophy to reflect on their hermeneutical assumptions. His provocative critiques were marked by unusual creativity; he not only deconstructed old ways of reading but also offered new ones. This is evident in his seminal work on Chandrakirti's *Madhyamakavatara*, which was published as *The Emptiness of Emptiness* (Hawaii UP, 1989). Sandy was also a gifted writer for non-academic audiences, making philosophical ideas accessible and rendering them with literary flair, as with his acclaimed novel, *Maya* (Wisdom Publications, 2015).

Sandy passed away peacefully on July 19, 2020, following a six-month struggle with pancreatic cancer. He is survived by Liz, his beloved wife of thirty-five years, and their two children, Sam and Katie.

About Wisdom Publications

Wisdom Publications is the leading publisher of classic and contemporary Buddhist books and practical works on mindfulness. To learn more about us or to explore our other books, please visit our website at wisdomexperience.org or contact us at the address below.

Wisdom Publications
199 Elm Street
Somerville, MA 02144 USA

We are a 501(c)(3) organization, and donations in support of our mission are tax deductible.

Wisdom Publications is affiliated with the Foundation for the Preservation of the Mahayana Tradition (FPMT).